THE SECRETS TO THE HEALING POWER

Principles of the Healing Power

Keith P. Hudson

The Place Where the Presence of God will Consume You!

THE SECRETS TO THE HEALING POWER

Principles of the Healing Power

Unless otherwise indicated, all Scripture quotations in this volume are from the King James Version of the Bible.

First Edition First Printing 2023

ISBN: 9798395313836

Your Contact Information:

Consuming Fire Christian Center
23310 Joy Road
Redford, Michigan 48239
(734) 266-2293
fire@consumingfirecc.org
https://www.consumingfirecc.org

Copyright © 2023 Keith P. Hudson
ALL RIGHTS ARE RESERVED.

No permission is given for any part of this book to be reproduced, transmitted in any form or means; electronic or mechanical, stored in a retrieval system, photocopied, recorded, scanned, or otherwise.

Any of these actions require the proper written permission of the author. The author hereby disclaims and does not assume liability for any injury, loss, damage, or disruption caused by errors or omissions, regardless of whether any errors or omissions result from negligence, accident, or any other cause. Readers are encouraged to verify any information contained in this book prior to taking any action on the information.

Referrals

"Pastor Keith Hudson is a man of the Holy Spirit. The presence and the power of God attends his ministry. Here is a man full of holiness and integrity! I have personally witnessed the miracle power of God through his life and ministry. What he is about to share with you are truths can trust and revelations that produce results! Many remarkable signs, wonders, and miracles of healing accompany the word of God that he preaches and teaches!!!"

~ Apostle Tony Kemp
President of the Acts Group/
Tony Kemp Ministries
Quincy, Illinois

I know Pastor Keith Personally and have witnessed firsthand the powerful healing anointing on his life. I know few others that carry such a strong tangible presence as they minister to the sick as he does. Pastor Keith has power with God.

~Apostle Marlin J. Reid
Senior Pastor
New Wine Glory Ministries - The River
Livonia, Michigan

"Love the books because sickness and disease are unmasked for what they are . Not just the old Pentecostal concept "of the devil ". You accurately present the role of sin self and the devil and consequently our mastery over sickness and demons through the power of faith, words, sounds, forgiveness, exercise, diet, sozo, deliverance etc. A really balanced and much needed approach. Well done !!!!"

~Apostle Fred Gulker
Senior Pastor
Shekinah Revival Ministries
Holland , Michigan

This book is a must. It teaches us how to be healed. Sickness/disease are consequences of Adams's sin. We must follow Natural laws. Learned about Emotional causes of disease A through W. Wow amazing awesome. We learn that intense emotions alter our health. The nervous system carries electrical signals. It's so true that our reality depends on what we think. It's important to know about the 17 hindrances to deliverance pg 30

It's an interesting fact that the spread of cancer skin cells can be detected by sound, wow! I enjoyed learning and reading about 32 major principles that must not be violated. And it's important to forgive, many are ill because of lack of forgiveness. Chapter 13 God's method of healing is a must. And the healing scriptures for specific parts of the body is handy to pray using appropriate for a specific body part. You end with the supernatural aftercare a much neglected part of the process.

> ~ **Apostle Wilford John Dilbert**
> **Iglesia Casa de Dios (House of God)**
> **Overseer Honduras Ministry**
> **56 churches in different villages and cities of Honduras.**
> **La Ceiba, Atlantida**

Preface

Good mental and physical health is God's plan for mankind. It never was God's intention for ailments, sickness, and diseases to enter the world He created.

These mental and physical infirmities continue to cost us a prosperous life. Our families, jobs, finances, emotional well-being and spiritual lives have been and continue to be impacted daily.

It is my heart's wish to add to information and books that have been written addressing God's heart's wish for everyone to be whole in their spirit, soul and body.

3 John 1:2 Beloved, I pray that in all things thou mayest prosper and be in health, even as thy soul prospereth.

We will explain some basic physical and scriptural applications that will position you to be healed and complete in spirit, soul and body.

To be successful you must be willing to develop habits and be consistent with the application of God's Word.

Those habits must include:

- A consistent relationship with God through Jesus Christ
- Meditating on the Word of God daily
- Acting on the Word meditated upon
- Believing that no Word from God is Void of Power. God can and will do what He declares.

We trust that the information contained herein will provide you with the information you need to receive your healing and also share with others – God's loving and merciful healing power.

Acknowledgment

All Glory, Honor and Worship belong to the KING OF KINGS, LORD OF LORDS - JESUS CHRIST

I want to acknowledge two men who help me in my spiritual walk in Christ. Apostle Marlin Reid, the Pastor of the River Church in Livonia, Michigan. He was the one who introduced me to Supernatural things of the Spirit.

Also, Apostle Tony Kemp took me under his wing and imparted in my life the Wisdom of God, the application of the Holy Spirit and the Word of God. God sent them into my life and helped me to desire more of God.

My wife, Bernadette and children – Stefan, Stacey and Sharita along with those who have been with me since the beginning of the Ministry in 2001.

James and Armelda Hudson
Melanie Staten
Miguel and Shunda Gonzales
Damon and Candice Luster
Charlotte Gailliard
Starla Marshall

Andre and Valerie Knight and family
Vincent and Cindy Warren and family
Roger and Sylvia Brown and family
Judy Heard
Regina Mills and family

Also, the Consuming Fire Christian Center's family, the greatest support down through the years.

I honor everyone, and I pray the prayer of Paul the Apostle to the Ephesian Church.

....cease not to give thanks for you, making mention of you in my prayers; that the God of our Lord Jesus Christ, the Father of glory, may give unto you a spirit of wisdom and revelation in the knowledge of him; having the eyes of your heart enlightened, that ye may know what is the hope of his calling, what the riches of the glory of his inheritance in the saints, and what the exceeding greatness of his power to us-ward who believe, according to that working of the strength of his might which he wrought in Christ, when he raised him from the dead, and made him to sit at his right hand in the heavenly places, far above all rule, and authority, and power, and dominion, and every name that is named, not only in this world, but also in that which is to come: and he put all things in subjection under his feet, and gave him to be head over all things to the church, which is his body, the fulness of him that filleth all in all. **Ephesian 1: 16-23**

Table of Contents

Chapter 1: The World in Pain 1

Chapter 2: The Laws of the Natural and Spiritual 5
    Sickness/Disease are consequences of Adam's sin. 6
    The Law of the Spirit 7
    The Law of the Natural 8
    The Relationship Between Emotions and Your Nervous System 10

Chapter 3: The Purpose of Sickness and Disease 15
    The characteristic of sickness and disease is to: 16
    Your body is a Living Organism 19

Chapter 4: The Sound 21
    Fundamental Key 22
    Here is an interesting fact: 22

Chapter 5: Principles of the Tares 26
    What are tares? 26

Chapter 6: Hindrance to Divine Healing 30
    Here is a list of hindrances to healing: 30

Chapter 7: The Major Principles that you Cannot Violate 32
    Principle One: No Word from God is Void of Power 32
    Principle Two: Take Care of Your Body 33
    Principle Three: Emotions 34

Chapter 8: The Demonic Realm 36

Chapter 9: The Power of Forgiveness 40

Chapter 10: How to Receive your Healing 43
    God's Redemption Plan includes Healing: 43
    There are three types of healing identified in the bible. 44
    Step 1 – Identify the illness, sickness or disease in the body and what part of the body. 46
    Step 2 – Do you know the source of the illness, sickness or disease? 46

Step 3 – Examination of the Heart 47
Step 4 – Meditate on and confess healing Scripture 48
Step 5 – Eat Healthy Food 49
Step 6 – Faith 49

Chapter 11: Meditate on the Word of God **50**

Chapter 12: Emotional Causes of Disease **53**
Emotional Causes of Disease Starting with A 53
Emotional Causes of Disease Starting with B 56
Emotional Causes of Disease Starting with C 58
Emotional Causes of Disease Starting with D 60
Emotional Causes of Disease Starting with E 61
Emotional Causes of Disease Starting with F 61
Emotional Causes of Diseases Starting with G 62
Emotional Causes of Diseases Starting with H 62
Emotional Causes of Diseases Starting with I 63
Emotional Causes of Diseases Starting with K 63
Emotional Causes of Diseases Starting with L 64
Emotional Causes of Diseases Starting with M 64
Emotional Causes of Diseases Starting with N 65
Emotional Causes of Diseases Starting with O 65
Emotional Causes of Diseases Starting with P 65
Emotional Causes of Diseases Starting with Q 67
Emotional Causes of Diseases Starting with R 67
Emotional Causes of Diseases Starting with S 68
Emotional Causes of Diseases Starting with T 70
Emotional Causes of Diseases Starting with U 71
Emotional Causes of Diseases Starting with V 71
Emotional Causes of Diseases Starting with W 71

Chapter 13: God's Methods of Healing **73**

Chapter 14: Healing Scriptures for Specific Body Parts **74**

Chapter 15: Supernatural Aftercare **97**
Maintain Your Healing and Deliverance 97
Tips on receiving and maintaining your healing and deliverance 98

Chapter 1
The World in Pain

For No Word from God shall be Void of Power.
— LUKE 1:37 ASV

Despite advanced technology and research in the medical field, more than at any other time in our history, people being diagnosed with sicknesses, ailments, and diseases has increased.

There are natural and spiritual solutions to obtain healing for the problems that ail us. The Bible provides a solution for sickness and diseases:

Genesis 1:28 And God blessed them, and God said unto them, Be fruitful, and multiply, and replenish the earth, and subdue it: and have dominion over the fish of the sea, and over the fowl of the air, and over every living thing that moveth upon the earth.

Genesis 1:29 And God said, Behold, I have given you every herb bearing seed, which is upon the face of all the earth, and every tree, in the which is the fruit of a tree yielding seed; to you it shall be for meat.

Mankind was made in the image of God, therefore our spiritual life and our natural existence are because of our Maker – God, who made everything that exists. But in order to live in the natural world that God gave us, we need a healthy environment, a healthy diet, and daily care for our bodies. Even though we do the best we can to live in a good environment, our surroundings can and do affect us.

We have more control over what we eat and how we maintain our bodies. God provided a basic natural diet for mankind before the fall in the Garden of Eden. The diet consisted of every herb bearing seed and tree which yields fruit. This diet was given with the intent for us to live and be sustained forever. Therefore, we must feed our bodies with healthy foods in our natural world to maintain our existence.

It was God's intention for mankind to live and thrive forever in the world He made for us. Due to the deception of the evil one (Satan), our world, our minds, and our bodies went under a curse. Our relationship with God was severed, causing us to lose our spiritual fellowship with God which included our health.

Genesis 3:9 And the LORD God called unto Adam, and said unto him, Where art thou?

Genesis 3:10 And he said, I heard thy voice in the garden, and I was afraid, because I was naked; and I hid myself.

Genesis 3:11 And he said, Who told thee that thou wast naked? Hast thou eaten of the tree, whereof I commanded thee that thou shouldest not eat?

Genesis 3:12 And the man said, The woman whom thou gavest to be with me, she gave me of the tree, and I did eat.

Genesis 3:13 And the LORD God said unto the woman, What is this that thou hast done? And the woman said, The serpent beguiled me, and I did eat.

Genesis 3:14 And the LORD God said unto the serpent, Because thou hast done this, thou art cursed above all cattle, and above every beast of the field; upon thy belly shalt thou go, and dust shalt thou eat all the days of thy life:

Genesis 3:15 And I will put enmity between thee and the woman, and between thy seed and her seed; it shall bruise thy head, and thou shalt bruise his heel.

Genesis 3:16 Unto the woman he said, I will greatly multiply thy sorrow and thy conception; in sorrow thou shalt bring forth children; and thy desire shall be to thy husband, and he shall rule over thee.

Genesis 3:17 And unto Adam he said, Because thou hast hearkened unto the voice of thy wife, and hast eaten of the tree, of which I commanded thee, saying, Thou shalt not eat of it: cursed is the ground for thy sake; in sorrow shalt thou eat of it all the days of thy life;

Genesis 3:18 Thorns also and thistles shall it bring forth thee; and thou shalt eat the herb of the field;

Genesis 3:19 In the sweat of thy face shalt thou eat bread, till thou return unto the ground; for out of it wast thou taken: for dust thou art, and unto dust shalt thou return.

However, the good news is:

Isaiah 53:5 But he was wounded for our transgressions, he was bruised for our iniquities: the chastisement of our peace was upon him; and with his stripes we are healed.

He was wounded for our transgression to repair the broken relationship that mankind violated.

He was bruised for our iniquities to repair and correct our wrong way of thinking and actions.

The chastisement of our peace was upon Him because He removed the penalty of judgment and eternal death upon us.

THE SECRET TO THE HEALING POWER

By His stripes we are healed, the stripes put on Him paid the price so we can be whole in spirit, soul, and body.

Through the finished work of Jesus Christ, He provided a way for us to be restored, repaired, and healed of every sickness, disease, pain, sorrow, rejection, etc. Christ, our Redeemer, and Healer (Jehovah Rapha).

It is our purpose to simplify the process for you so that you can receive healing for your body, soul, and spirit.

Chapter 2
The Laws of the Natural and Spiritual

The first thing we need to understand is that there are two laws that we live by; the Law of the natural and the Law of the Spirit. An understanding of these laws are essential. They work hand-in-hand in almost all cases when it comes to healing the soul and body

When God created mankind, there was no sickness, disease, pain, or misery. All of these came after the fall of man. Before the fall of mankind God established spiritual and natural laws that govern our eternal life on Earth. These two laws, The Law of the Spirit and The Law of the natural (nature) operated in harmony until the fall of mankind in the Garden of Eden. If either of these laws are broken, they can cause separation and thereby produce sickness, disease, mental and emotional conditions – a corrupt nature that causes defects in our souls and bodies. These conditions are contrary to God's intention for mankind.

Sickness/Disease are consequences of Adam's sin.

God told Adam, "The day you eat of the tree of the knowledge of good and evil you will surely die." Death is a consequence of sin **(Romans 6:23)**. Sickness and disease are the agents of death used to destroy people's lives.

Sickness and disease can come upon every one of us. It can be through:

- **Generational Curses** (disease/ sickness) passed down through generations.
- **Natural Environment** – viruses, bacteria, chemicals.
- **Weak immunity system** – unhealthy eating habits and stress.
- **Emotions that cause stress** – the trauma of the past, the inability to let things go, and unforgiveness.
- **One's mindset** – what a person thinks about themselves
- **Demons** – due to sin, witchcraft, rituals of the occult, spells, etc.

As you examine the list, you can see that there are things that are natural and spiritual. There are some scripture references in the latter pages of this book that can help us identify some reasons for sicknesses and diseases that come upon us.

Mankind broke fellowship with God by disobedience, and the law of the spirit was broken. Therefore, the doorway of sickness and disease was introduced to the human family.

Natural laws are for creation, whereas spiritual laws are for the spirit and soul. Creation is relative and material. The spirit and soul are not seen by natural eyes but affect what your body does.

Psalms 38:3 There is no soundness in my flesh because of thine anger; neither is there any rest in my bones **because of my sin**.

Hebrews 12:15 Looking diligently lest any man fail of the grace of God; lest any **root of bitterness** springing up trouble you, and thereby many be defiled.

The Law of the Spirit

The Word of God declares in **Romans 8:2** "For the law of the Spirit of life in Christ Jesus hath made me free from the law of sin and death."

When man disobeyed God, he altered his body, environment, the world, and everything in it; quickly cutting himself off from God's presence, power, protection, and life. Now he is no longer living in God but separate from Him; which caused spiritual death to come instantly, essentially becoming "a walking dead man."

The Law of the Spirit of Life is defined as being born again and having received the Holy Spirit in your life. By regeneration, we receive divine and eternal life in our spirit. It purges us of the penalty of death along with sickness and disease. This law liberates us from the law of sin and death and provides us access to the benefits of the Finished Work of Jesus Christ. This includes but is not limited to divine healing. The Law of the Spirit provides us with protection and the benefits of healing in the body, soul, and spirit.

God made us be like Him. This means we are designed to reflect God in our life. To reflect God is to do what He does. Our character should be like His, our deeds should be like His, our speech should be like His, we should think and act like Him in every area of our life. Just like a shadow boxer, we should do everything that the original does.

As a result of reflecting God, God in turn, shadows us. This means we become one with Him and nothing can overtake us as long as we stay in His shadow. We must live in the abiding presence of **_Jehovah – Rapha!_**

Psalms 91:1 He that dwelleth in the secret place of the Most High shall abide under the shadow of the Almighty.

Psalms 91:2 I will say of the LORD, He is my refuge and my fortress: my God; in him will I trust.

Psalms 91:3 Surely, he shall deliver thee from the snare of the fowler, and from the noisome pestilence.

Psalms 91:4 He shall cover thee with his feathers, and under his wings shalt thou trust: his truth shall be thy shield and buckler.

Psalms 91:5 Thou shalt not be afraid for the terror by night; nor for the arrow that flieth by day;

Psalms 91:6 Nor for the pestilence that walketh in darkness; nor for the destruction that wasteth at noonday.

Psalms 91:7 A thousand shall fall at thy side, and ten thousand at thy right hand; but it shall not come nigh thee.

As long as mankind walked with the VOICE of God, man was free; sickness and disease did not exist!

Genesis 3:8 And they heard the voice of the LORD God walking in the garden in the cool of the day: ....

The Law of the Natural

The Bible tells us that there are laws of nature: "ordinances of heaven and earth" (Jeremiah 33:25). There are no exceptions to these laws; every animal, plant, rock, a particle of matter, even the light waves, are all bound by these laws. These laws describe the way God normally accomplishes His creation in the universe and on the earth.

God's logic is the foundation for the universe. Therefore, the universe or anything in it cannot be considered haphazard or arbitrary. Even the universe operates according to some laws, particularly laws of chemistry that are logically derived from the laws of physics.

Many of these can be derived from the laws of mathematics. The basis of all these scientific laws is God's logic being discovered by man. These laws are the logical and orderly way the Lord upholds and sustains the universe. These laws are like pillars that He has created. Laws of nature are perfectly consistent with the biblical creation of the universe. In fact, the Bible simply states that God is the foundation for natural laws. Everything comes from Him by His Word and Holy Spirit.

God created the human body to function according to natural laws. Before the fall of mankind, the human body was perfect in every way. Each system had a specific function, which was carried out flawlessly.

Each one of these systems in our body is connected to our emotions and mind. Recent research shows that you can consciously choose to influence the development of your mind and emotions. It has been discovered that your heart functions as a complex information and networking center.

In the book The Biology of Belief, cellular biologist Bruce Lipton, Ph.D., shares current biomedical research about how your beliefs become your biology. With each heartbeat, your heart communicates with your body, heart, and brain through your nervous system, hormonal system, electromagnetic fields, and other energetic pathways. These internal communication networks also affect the way you perceive your reality which greatly influences the emotions you experience. Your emotions are perfectly reflected in your nervous system. Scientific research shows that your emotions stimulate very specific activities in your nervous system. This means that your nervous system has the intelligence to distinguish between positive and negative emotions. It has been discovered that intense emotions are clearly shown in your heart's rhythms.

For example, when you are experiencing intense emotions like fear, frustration, anxiety or anger, your heart rhythms are spiked and jagged and because there is a neural (nerve) connection between your heart and brain, your intense emotions greatly affect your ability to think clearly. However, the opposite also is true whenever you feel loved and appreciated. As you generate internal feelings of emotional well-being and your heart rhythms become synchronized and harmonious and your ability to think clearly is enhanced.

The Relationship Between Emotions and Your Nervous System

The following article was written by Dr. Andrew Weil. He is the *Founder and Director/Professor of Medicine and Public Health/ Lovell-Jones Endowed Chair in Integrative Medicine.*

Let's look at some of the inner workings of your nervous system's structure and how it communicates with your heart, brain and body. The nervous system is your body's primary communication network. Your nerves, like wires, carry electrical signals or messages within and between all the parts of your body. You have conscious or voluntary control over the sensory and motor systems of your central nervous system.

The sensory branch of your central nervous system receives and transmits information from the outside world through your five senses (sound, sight, smell, taste and touch) to your brain. So, you can perceive the physical world around you while the motor branch of your central nervous system carries internal signals from your brain to your body, making it possible for you to walk, talk and perform actions in the world around you. It is your autonomic nervous system that is the autonomic branch of your nervous system and is non-conscious or involuntary, meaning you have no apparent control over its function. Your autonomic nervous system operates at a subconscious level to control all the functions of your internal organs and glands which secrete hormones involved in your ability to feel emotions. There are long-standing assumptions about emotions that explain how your body always perfectly mirrors your unconscious thought patterns, the internal story you tell yourself, and how your body speaks to you through your emotions. In fact, your emotions are the language of your subconscious mind. Your autonomic nervous system has two branches of activity. The sympathetic (fight/flight) branch speeds up your heart rate as it signals you to prepare for action, and the parasympathetic (relaxation) branch slows down heart rate as it signals you for rest and recovery. Different types of emotions send different messages through your nervous system to the heart, brain and body. You can feel your emotions rush through your body like cascading waves of energy. Constant streams of intense emotions like fear, frustration and anger are known to overtax your autonomic nervous system with stress signals, causing its neural networks to jam. This is analogous to driving with one foot on the gas pedal while the other is on the brake.

Eventually, a chronic build-up of stress leads to autonomic nervous system imbalance; a state of chaos within your autonomic nervous system which results in your stress response getting stuck and remaining in the "on" position for fight or flight. The autonomic nervous system is known to stimulate your hormonal production and response. Autonomic nervous system balance is an essential key to healthy functioning of the body, mind and emotions. Prolonged stress commonly is recognized as the primary cause of disease and premature death. "Vegetative dystony" is the term used to describe autonomic nervous system imbalance and its accompanying symptoms. Manifestations of autonomic nervous system imbalance include common symptoms of headache, hot flashes, irregular heartbeat, nervousness, depression and anxiety.

According to Dr. Andrew Weil, medical vocabulary for imbalances of the autonomic nervous system practically does not exist in North American medicine. However, both Germany and Japan,

THE SECRET TO THE HEALING POWER

two modern-day industrial giants, acknowledge the condition and use the term "vegetative dystony." Our modern-day lifestyle promotes our living in a chronic condition of stress and being subjected to an increasing array of environmental toxins. These two conditions are cited as primary causes of autonomic nervous system imbalance and resulting hormonal disturbances. The most potent antidote for overcoming autonomic nervous system imbalance is simple: Give yourself a nourishing diet of regularly feeling positive and uplifting emotions such as appreciation, love and compassion to signal your nervous system to relax and promote an internal environment of peace and harmony. The most effective way is to read and meditate on the Word of God daily to fight off stress and negative emotions. Your positive emotions effectively allow the two branches of your autonomic nervous system to sync with each other. Then your body's glands and organs will work together in harmony and your heart's rhythms will become synchronized and harmonious. Dr. Candace Pert calls these signals that your subconscious mind sends through your autonomic nervous system the "molecules of your emotions."

This information is parallel to the Word of God that indicates:

Proverb 23:7 For as he thinketh in his heart, so is he: Eat and drink, saith he to thee; but his heart is not with thee.

Proverb 18:21 Death and life are in the power of the tongue: and they that love it shall eat the fruit thereof.

Your reality is what you think, believe, and say about yourself, your body, and your life. Therefore, your influence can either be – God's thinking, man's thinking, or Satan's thinking about yourself and how it concerns your life. These can affect one or more of these body systems indicated below:

- Circulatory system
- Digestive system
- Endocrine system
- Lymphatic system
- Muscular system

- Nervous system
- Respiratory system
- Skeletal system
- Reproductive system
- Urinary system

Each one of the systems in the body is tied to your emotions. Additionally, if your emotions are negative, it will affect the respective system of the body.

An example of this which is common is back problems.

Back problems can be a result of one of the following; which is attached to your emotions:

If a person is feeling a lack of emotional support or feeling unloved, they will feel upper back pain or have upper back problems. If a person is having lower back problems, it can be a feeling of a lack of financial support or concerns.

Let me indicate that this may not be the case in every situation, but it is common enough that doctors and mental health care experts are now addressing it.

Psalms 139:14 I will praise thee; for I am fearfully and wonderfully made: marvelous are thy works; and that my soul knoweth right well.

Hebrews 2:6 But one in a certain place testified, saying, what is man, that thou art mindful of him? or the son of man, that thou visitest him?

Hebrews 2:7 Thou madest him a little lower than the angels; thou crownedst him with glory and honour, and didst set him over the works of thy hands:

However, man violated the natural law of God through disobedience, and the laws were altered. This curse affects mankind's food supply, thereby upsetting the natural balance and ability to live a full, and natural life.

THE SECRET TO THE HEALING POWER

Instead of the ground yielding to mankind, the ground now had to be worked. Man had to tilt the ground for him to eat. The ground was cursed, which means the plants and fruits from the earth would die also without someone caring for them.

Genesis 3:17 ...cursed is the ground for thy sake; in sorrow shalt thou eat of it all the days of thy life;

Genesis 3:18 Thorns also and thistles shall it bring forth to thee; and thou shalt eat the herb of the field;

Genesis 3:19 In the sweat of thy face shalt thou eat bread, till thou return unto the ground; for out of it wast thou taken: for dust thou art, and unto dust shalt thou return.

Chapter 3
The Purpose of Sickness and Disease

Sickness is defined as a condition of being in bad health or impairment of normal physiological function affecting part or the entirety of an organism.

From the Greek definition, it is defined as strengthless (in various applications, literally, or figuratively and morally): – more feeble, impotent, sick, without strength, weak (-er, -ness, thing).

Disease is defined as any malfunctioning of host cells and tissues that results from continuous irritation by a pathogenic agent or environmental factor and leads to the development of symptoms. A condition of the body in which; there is incorrect functioning due to heredity, infection, diet, or environment.

In the Greek definition, it is defined as; an ailment: – disease.

The function of sickness and disease is to cause your organs or body to malfunction. They destroy or weaken the body by attacking or taking nutrition from healthy cells. There must be a suitable environment for the malfunctioning cells to reproduce and grow.

The characteristic of sickness and disease is to:

- Weaken the organs or body
- Cause malfunctioning, or stops the functioning of organs or specific parts of the body
- Attack foreign pathogenic bodies known as a cell, parasites, or viruses on the organs or body

The Bible declares this in **Deuteronomy 28:15-68**. If we look at the verses, which are the curses of the law, it describes three areas of life that mankind can be affected in:

- The human body
- The mental and emotional state
- The financial and living life

Sickness, disease, mental illness, pain, rejection, misery, etc., are the consequence of the fallen mankind. The effect of sickness and disease is to destroy a person's life. This is the process that the enemy has implemented in **St. John 10:10**.

The thief cometh not, but for to steal, and to kill, and to destroy: I am come that they might have life, and that they might have it more abundantly. **St. John 10:10.**

The word "steal" in Greek is "keptī" – and it is defined as taking something from a person that is owned by that person or in his/her legal possession.

Sickness is likened to a picture of a thief that uses deception, deceit, mischievous skill, or a cunning way to take something from you without your knowledge; until it is gone. It is also illustrated by using the analogy of a thief who gained access to a place by burglary or breaking in forcefully because the locks are not strong enough. The thief breaks in unlawfully to take what he wants.

So, ask yourself a few questions:

1. Is my health watched and guarded?
2. Do I value my health (is it a treasure)?

3. Do I practice what the Word of God says regarding my health?

The word "kill" is very interesting. It has 25 Greek definitions (615, 5407, 2380, 337, 1315, 2695, 914, 3970, 4372, 2818, 336, 4969, 1205, 2289, 2419, 4983, 290, 4618, 443, 4501, 622, 3448, 1388, 1202, 2548).

The definition used is 2380, which is "thuō"," to slay or slaughter for a sacrifice. The illustration is to take an object of sacrifice and slaughter it.

I believe the enemy wants to take our Godly and righteous life from us and put it on a demonic altar and offer us as a sacrifice for the enemy's glory and not God's glory.

The last word is "destroy" and in Greek, it is "apollumi." It is defined as abolishing, putting an end to, to ruin, rendering useless, and declaring that one must be put to death.

The illustration is that you become useless enough to qualify to be put to death.

In summary, the enemy wants to take part, if not all of what you legally own; your health, your Godliness, your faith, your living sacrifice to God, your ministry, etc. It wants to make your life a demonic sacrifice for his glory and as a result, you lose your eternal life with God.

He does this by first stealing your faith and trust in God. One of his many methods is getting us to take our guard down. Then we begin to lose our faith and start questioning God, as though He did something to us.

The real truth of the matter is this. God doesn't bring or put sickness upon us. Sickness and disease come as a result of mankind's broken covenant with God because of Adam. Because of the broken covenant, evil and death exist, and sickness and disease are their agents.

THE SECRET TO THE HEALING POWER

Deuteronomy 28:15 But it shall come to pass, if thou wilt not hearken unto the voice of the LORD thy God, to observe to do all his commandments and his statutes which I command thee this day; that all these curses shall come upon thee, and overtake thee:

Deuteronomy 28:20 The LORD shall send upon thee cursing, vexation, and rebuke, in all that thou set test thine hand unto for to do, until thou be destroyed, and until thou perish quickly; because of the wickedness of thy doings, whereby thou hast forsaken me.

Deuteronomy 28:24 The LORD shall make the rain of thy land powder and dust: from heaven shall it come down upon thee, until thou be destroyed.

Deuteronomy 28:51 And he shall eat the fruit of thy cattle, and the fruit of thy land, until thou be destroyed: which also shall not leave thee either corn, wine, or oil, or the increase of thy kin, or flocks of thy sheep, until he has destroyed thee.

Deuteronomy 28:61 Also every sickness, and every plague, which is not written in the book of this law, them will the LORD bring upon thee, until thou be destroyed.

Satan is the god of this world and prince of the air; therefore, he blinds people's minds from the truth. The evil one influences the thoughts of mankind negatively. Satan is the one causing sickness and disease in the world, generational sickness/diseases, demonic attacks on the body, viruses, environments, etc.

Corinthians 4:4 In whom the god of this world hath blinded the minds of them which believe not, lest the light of the glorious gospel of Christ, who is the image of God, should shine unto them.

Thank God that Jesus came to destroy sickness and disease in our lives. What Jesus did on Calvary prepared us for the benefits of healing in body, soul, and spirit.

Luke 5:12 And it came to pass, when he was in a certain city, behold a man full of leprosy: who seeing Jesus fell on his face, and besought him, saying, Lord, if thou wilt, thou canst make me clean.

Luke 5:13 And he put forth his hand, and touched him, saying, I will: be thou clean. And immediately the leprosy departed from him.

St. John 10:10 I am come that they might have life, and that they might have it more abundantly.

John 1:2 Beloved, I wish above all things that thou mayest prosper and be in health, even as thy soul prosperity.

Galatians 3:13 Christ hath redeemed us from the curse of the law, being made a curse for us: for it is written, Cursed is every one that hanged on a tree:

Exodus 23:25 And ye shall serve the LORD your God, and he shall bless thy bread, and thy water; and I will take sickness away from the midst of thee.

Exodus 23:26 There shall nothing cast their young, nor be barren, in thy land: the number of thy days I will fulfil.

As a believer in Jesus, our newly-born spirit man (the spirit we receive by accepting Jesus as Lord and Savior of our life) should govern our soul (mind and thinking) and thereby direct our body. We can establish this pattern in our life by developing Godly habits that will always bring Godly results. In this case, supernatural health, divine maintenance, and healing occur.

Your body is a Living Organism

Every cell has a character, function, purpose, and destiny. To better understand this statement, let's examine the characteristics of cancer cells. When the environment in the body is out of balance, cells begin to mutate thereby resulting in the formation of a cancer cell. This cell begins to multiply and spread, taking over healthy cells. After attacking healthy cells, if unmanaged, or managed poorly, cancer can begin to attack organs, eventually shutting them down. In time, if unchecked, cancer will spread to multiple organs, affecting the functioning of the entire body. Once the cancer cells are established, their purpose is to first survive, multiply, and ultimately destroy the cells that it comes in contact with. Cancer is but one sickness out of the many sicknesses in existence and those yet to be discovered.

The good news is that every cell is still subject to the creator of all things! We have access to the keys to conquering every sickness and disease through the healing power of the Almighty God.

Every cell can hear it and as a result, when it hears the Word from the Creator of all things, it will respond accordingly.

Chapter 4
The Sound

Understanding and possessing the knowledge that all things were created by the voice of God through His Spirit, we have the power to unlock the secrets of divine healing for both body and soul. In Genesis chapter 1, we find what could be considered one of the most magnificent and powerful phrases in all of God's words, "And God said..." When God "said"... things happen.

Sound is the basis of all life. Our bodies, our spirit, and souls came into existence because of God's breath. God breathed His Word into man and he became a living soul

Genesis 2:7 And the LORD God formed man of the dust of the ground, and breathed into his nostrils the breath of life; and man became a living soul.

God's Word is the audible stream of energy that comes from the heart of God. It is the spiritual energy through which a person returns to the heart of God. Sound current is mentioned or studied in many religions. In the Bible, it is referred to as "the Word".

Fundamental Key

St. John 1:1 In the beginning was the Word, and the Word was with God, and the Word was God.

St. John 1:2 The same was in the beginning with God.

St. John 1:3 All things were made by him; and without him was not anything made that was made.

Hebrew 11:3 Through faith we understand that the worlds were framed by the word of God, so that things which are seen were not made of things which do appear.

Sound is defined as a disturbance of mechanical energy that propagates through matter as a longitudinal wave and therefore is a mechanical wave. Sound is characterized by the properties of sound waves, which are frequency, wave length, period, amplitude and speed.

Here is an interesting fact:

WASHINGTON, Oct. 16 – Researchers at the University of Missouri-Columbia can now detect the spread of skin cancer cells through the blood by literally listening to their sounds. The unprecedented, minimally invasive technique causes melanoma cells to emit noise and can allows oncologists to spot early signs of metastases – as few as 10 cancer cells in a blood sample before they even settle in other organs. The results of the successful experimental tests appeared in the Oct. 15 issue of the journal Optics Letters, published by the Optical Society of America.

Paper: "Photoacoustic detection of metastatic melanoma cells in the human circulatory system," by Ryan M. Weight, John A. Viator, Paul S. Dale, Charles W. Caldwell, and Allison E. Lisle, Optics Letters, Vol. 31, Issue 20, pp. 2998-3000.

This offers one example of how sound functions and operates.

The Word of God is God's thoughts spoken forth.

St. John 1:1 In the beginning was the Word, and the Word was with God, and the Word was God.

Isaiah 55:11 So shall my word be that goeth forth out of my mouth: it shall not return unto me void, but it shall accomplish that which I please, and it shall prosper in the thing whereto I sent it.

The sound of God's voice is creative and powerful. This is evident in the book of Genesis. The phrase "And God said..." was followed by creative action. When God speaks a Word, His thoughts, it begins to form into reality. The sound of God's voice and His Word by his Spirit is and has been the greatest form of creation. The bible tells us that the Word of God is so powerful that God watches it to ensure it is performed and He even puts it above His name!

Psalms 138:2 I will worship toward thy holy temple, and praise thy name for thy lovingkindness and for thy truth: for thou hast magnified thy word above all thy name.

To understand the secrets to the sound of God, first, we must understand the laws of the Spirit through Jesus Christ in order to obtain our healing in Christ.

Number One – understand that everything that was made or created in the universe comes from the voice of God, which is His sound, which is His Word.

Number Two – understand that everything is made from the Word of God, and it was created by the sound pattern of God. Understand that the sound patterns or the Word of God provides access to divine healing.

Number Three – understand that in order to experience God's ability to heal, create and restore, we must duplicate or mimic God's Word or sound pattern.

THE SECRET TO THE HEALING POWER

Number Four – understand that since everything was made by the sound of God's Word, His Word is alive and there is a response to the voice of God's Word when spoken.

Sound is simply the reflection of its patterns or waves. The length or frequency of the wave determines the effect it will have. When someone speaks, another person can hear. Glass responds to an extremely high- frequency sound wave by shattering. God's Word is no different. When a word is spoken, based on the Word or pattern of God, it can affect, create or change whatever God is speaking to. The key is matching the word to the circumstance. Here are a few examples, out of the Word of God.

Acts 3:3 Who seeing Peter and John about to go into the temple asked alms.

Acts 3:4 And Peter, fastening his eyes upon him with John, said, Look on us.

Acts 3:5 And he gave heed unto them, expecting to receive something of them.

Acts 3:6 Then Peter said, Silver and gold have I none; but such as I have give I thee: In the name of Jesus Christ of Nazareth rise up and walk.

Acts 3:7 And he took him by the right hand, and lifted him up: and immediately his feet and ankle bones received strength.

St. John 11:41 Then they took away the stone from the place where the dead was laid. And Jesus lifted up his eyes, and said, Father, I thank thee that thou hast heard me.

St. John 11:42 And I knew that thou hearest me always: but because of the people which stand by I said it, that they may believe that thou hast sent me.

St. John 11:43 And when he thus had spoken, he cried with a loud voice, Lazarus, come forth.

St. John 11:44 And he that was dead came forth, bound hand and foot with graveclothes: and his face was bound about with a napkin. Jesus saith unto them, Loose him, and let him go.

Luke 5:16 And he withdrew himself into the wilderness, and prayed.

Luke 5:17 And it came to pass on a certain day, as he was teaching, that there were Pharisees and doctors of the law sitting by, which were come out of every town of Galilee, and Judaea, and Jerusalem: and the power of the Lord was present to heal them.

These examples illustrate how powerful the Word of God is when the conditions are right. In order to receive we must prepare.

Chapter 5
Principles of the Tares

Some principles govern the laws of God's Word and if those principles are ignored it is the reason why we don't receive our expectations. These principles focus on our lack of faith and abundance of unbelief. This is what I call TARES.

What are Tares?

Tares, sometimes called ryegrasses, like many other cool-season kinds of grasses, are often infected by a clandestine fungal entophyte that lives symbiotically within its leaves. Some species, particularly temulentum, are weeds that can have a severe impact on the production of wheat and other crops.

Spiritually, tares are our belief in the world systems and other thoughts that are in direct opposition to God's Word and can infect our ability to believe God's Word.

In the parable of the Tares in **Matthew 13:24-30**, good seed and tares were sowed in the ground. They begin to grow together infecting the good crop that would be harvested one day. Both plants are fed from their respective sources but the tares are infected.

The good seed is feeding on the Word of God, while the tares are feeding on the world system and other thoughts. Remember, the tares are infected and can spread their infection to the good seed as they begin to grow. The infection can hinder or even stop the growth and kill some of the good seeds.

1 Corinthians 15:33 Be not deceived: evil communications corrupt good manners.

Years and years of being educated in the world system have filled our minds with untruths and false hope. We have nourished the tares of our hearts for too long! When it is time to believe God for His promises, His healing, His provisions, and other benefits promised to us, our faith struggles because it has been infected.

We must change the way we think and speak. When we talk about sickness and disease, we may say, "Uncle Joe Apple died from cancer," so we automatically believe that cancer will overcome us. When we suffer from a cold or the flu our first thought is going to the doctor's office for a prescription. When we get a headache, we search the nearest medicine cabinet for some technologically advanced drug.

Once sickness comes to us with no relief from the doctors, technology, or medicines, that is when we recognize God's help. Our minds are engulfed in the patterns of the world systems and sometimes it is hard to believe the Word of God.

Most of us are accustomed to the experience of speaking God's Word with no results. This is an effect of the doubt cast in our minds by the world systems. However, when you begin to sow your faith by hearing the Word, your doubt begins to decrease.

Romans 10:17 So then faith cometh by hearing, and hearing by the word of God.

In order for the Word of God to operate in our lives, we must outgrow the tares, we must transition from believing to knowing. There is no doubt concerning what God's Word says about your circumstances. In fact, you must live by or be a reflection of your beliefs! Your lifestyle must be a reflection of what God has promised.

God's Word works on the principles of faith, confession, and action.

What we feed is what grows and what we feed on is what we become. Therefore, we must feed our faith and starve our doubt. We must starve the worldly way of thinking from our hearts and begin to replicate God's thoughts and words.

The seed of the Word of God must be in your heart and grow until it matures in you. It must penetrate your heart and become part of you. The tares have to be uprooted and removed from our thoughts.

Mark 9:24 ...and said with tears, Lord, I believe; help thou mine unbelief.

Matthew 17:19 Then came the disciples to Jesus apart, and said, Why could not we cast him out?

Matthew 17:20 And Jesus said unto them, Because of your unbelief: for verily I say unto you, if ye have faith as a grain of mustard seed, ye shall say unto this mountain, Remove hence to yonder place; and it shall remove; and nothing shall be impossible unto you.

Matthews 17:21 Howbeit this kind goeth not out but by prayer and fasting.

God's Word has provided a simple way of ridding the tares in our life by fervent prayer and fasting. Prayer provides direct communication to the Father and fasting eliminates the effect of the flesh and reduces the influence of the world system. As the influence of your flesh and mind on your soul begins to weaken, the spirit man in you will be strengthened and operate in its divine nature. The divine nature is God's character. Your spirit man will begin to repeat the declarations that are in God's Word. As your spirit man becomes stronger it will begin to pattern itself after the Spirit of God. The spirit man will hear, see and know the mind of the Spirit.

Romans 8:5 For they that are after the flesh do mind the things of the flesh; but they that are after the Spirit the things of the Spirit.

Romans 8:27 And he that searcheth the hearts knoweth what is the mind of the Spirit, because he maketh intercession for the saints according to the will of God.

Let's put it in perspective.

- We must believe that God is able to heal us and he has made the power readily available through His Word.
- We must hear the Word of God and feed our spirit man by meditation. **(Joshua 1:8)**
- We must eliminate all doubt by fasting and praying according to the Word of God.
- We must begin to speak as God speaks.

Joshua 1:8 This book of the law shall not depart out of thy mouth; but thou shalt meditate therein day and night, that thou mayest observe to do according to all that is written therein: for then thou shalt make thy way prosperous, and then thou shalt have good success.

Psalms 1:2 But his delight is in the law of the LORD; and in his law doth he meditate day and night.

Chapter 6
Hindrance to Divine Healing

Here is a list of hindrances to healing:

Hindrance 1: Testing God's ability. **Luke 23:8, Matthew 27:42, Hebrews 11:6**

Hindrance 2: Wanting signs more than God's promises. **John 5:2-3, John 5:6, John 4:48**

Hindrance 3: Trusting doctors more than God. **Luke 8:43, 2 Chronicles 16:12-13**

Hindrance 4: Sinning against God. **1 Corinthians 5:1, 4-5, 2 Corinthians 2:6-7**

Hindrance 5: Unconfessed sins involving others. **James 5:16**

Hindrance 6: Unforgiveness. **Mark 11:25-26, Job 42:10**

Hindrance 7: Fear. **Job 3:25**

Hindrance 8: Focusing on circumstances and symptoms. **Matthew 14:28-30**

Hindrance 9: Looking for healing instead of divine health. **Exodus 23:25**

Hindrance 10: Our time on earth is over. **2 Kings 13:14, 2 Kings 20:1**

Hindrance 11: Disregarding your body. **1 Corinthians 6:19-20**

Hindrance 12: Impatience. **2 Peter 3:15**

Hindrance 13: Not building up your faith. **Romans 10:17, Romans 12:12**

Hindrance 14: Lack of Prayer and fasting. **Mark 9:29**

Hindrance 15: Lack of understanding of Christ's atonement. **1 Peter 2:24**

Hindrance 16: Ignoring God's ministries in the church. **1 Corinthians 11:29-30**

Hindrance 17: Not believing in God's promises.

Chapter 7
The Major Principles that you Cannot Violate

Nature and Spiritual principles work in harmony, and produce results. The following are the two principles that work together:

Principle One: No Word from God is Void of Power

There are two things about God that you should know. God does not lie, and His character does not change!

Hebrews 6:13 For when God made promise to Abraham, because he could swear by no greater, he sware by himself,

Hebrews 6:14 Saying, Surely blessing I will bless thee, and multiplying I will multiply thee.

Hebrews 6:15 And so, after he had patiently endured, he obtained the promise.

Hebrews 6:16 For men verily swear by the greater: and an oath for confirmation is to them an end of all strife.

Hebrews 6:17 Wherein God, willing more abundantly to shew unto the heirs of promise the immutability of his counsel, confirmed it by an oath:

Hebrews 6:18 That by two immutable things, in which it was impossible for God to lie, we might have a strong consolation, who have fled for refuge to lay hold upon the hope set before us:

Hebrews 13:8 Jesus Christ the same yesterday, and today, and forever.

Romans 10:8 But what saith it? The word is nigh thee, even in thy mouth, and in thy heart: that is, the word of faith, which we preach;

By confessing the Word continually, you set in motion the pattern of God's Word, repeating the sound that heals, creates, and restores.

Principle Two: Take Care of Your Body

Our bodies are the temples in which God dwells, therefore, we are required to care for them. God uses our bodies to accomplish His work. If your body is not in excellent condition, you limit God's ability to work through you. As in the beginning, God designed our bodies to function properly. Therefore, we need to eat the right foods, exercise, and get the proper rest. Our bodies have been designed to live on earth, not in glory.

It has been scientifically proven that organic foods are the best for us. Such food may not be as pure as it was in the Garden of Eden, but it is the best we can have.

Today, organic food is produced by farmers who emphasize the use of renewable resources and the conservation of soil and water to enhance environmental quality for future generations. Organic meat, poultry, eggs, and dairy products come from animals that are given no antibiotics or growth hormones. Organic food is produced without using most conventional pesticides such as fertilizers made with synthetic ingredients or sewage sludge, bioengineering, or ionizing radiation. Before a product can be labeled "organic", a government-approved certifier inspects the farm where the food is grown to make sure the farmer is following all the rules necessary to meet USDA organic standards.

The Bible identifies and recognizes good and healthy diets. God spoke to Israel regarding what to eat and what not to eat in Leviticus, Chapter 11, and Deuteronomy, Chapter 14. As you observe what God told Israel to eat, you will find that it has been proven that these things are healthy and beneficial for the body.

1 Corinthians 6:19 What? know ye not that your body is the temple of the Holy Ghost which is in you, which ye have of God, and ye are not your own?

1 Timothy 4:8 For bodily exercise profiteth little: but godliness is profitable unto all things, having promise of the life that now is, and of that which is to come.

Principle Three: Emotions

If you are not careful, you can begin to develop negative thoughts towards other people without understanding that while these thoughts have absolutely no effect on the other person whatsoever, they do affect you. That is why Jesus went to such great extents to teach us to turn the other cheek. This was not simply a teaching. If someone asks you to walk one mile, walk two. If someone asks for your coat, give them your cloak. If they hit you on one cheek, give them the other side. The whole premise of this teaching was freedom and reliance on God. True freedom is found when it is God who is in control, and not people, events, or circumstances. This attitude frees us from animosity, hatred, aggravation, ill-will, grief, sorrow, pain, and suffering which can poison and destroy our emotions, minds, and physical body. Jesus gave this wisdom in one simple teaching and showed us how to become free from these things.

Just as our thoughts can make us ill, they can also help us to heal. Meditation on God's Word can provide an imagery of you being complete and whole in mind and body. There is growing clinical evidence that imagery is beneficial in treating skin disease, diabetes, breast cancer, arthritis, headaches, and severe burns. Jesus taught us in Mark that "Whatever you ask for in prayer, believe that you have received it, and it will be yours." Today is a good day to begin to pray in faith to see yourself resting in God for a positive outcome and to start to change your life as you get freedom from poisonous thoughts.

Hebrews 12:15 Looking diligently lest any man fail of the grace of God; lest any root of bitterness springing up trouble you, and thereby many be defiled;

Chapter 8
The Demonic Realm

Many people don't believe in the demonic realm and how it can affect the natural realm. Demonic spiritual beings operate by a universal spiritual law. God has given every spiritual being He created "Choice." Choice is the power, right, or liberty to choose, to have options.

The Bible tells us in **Revelation 3:20** that Jesus Himself will stand before us and knock on our doors to see if we will be willing to open up that door and allow Him to come into our lives. In **St. John 13:2 and 28**, Judas Iscariot allowed Satan to place a thought in his mind to betray Jesus. Judas' betrayal happened because of negative thoughts in his heart after becoming disappointed in Jesus' ministry. The Jewish people believed the prophecy that a Messiah was coming to conquer the Roman Empire through a war that would set the Jewish people free from their oppression. Judas wanted the Roman government overthrown because it was oppressing the Jewish people but Jesus came and showed love toward everyone, even to the Romans. He gave money to the poor and fellowshipped with sinners.

This was very disappointing to Judas. He became disheartened with Jesus ministry and satan put thoughts in Judas' heart to betray Jesus.

Once he accepted the thoughts of betrayal, the doorway of the demonic was opened. Satan was allowed to enter the door of Judas' heart because of the disappointments. Thoughts result in actions.

In order to have Jesus come into our lives, we must be willing to give Him permission to enter our lives. God will never force Himself on any of us. He will let us know He wants to come into our lives. He will always knock at the door of our hearts, but we have to decide whether or not we are willing to open up that door and allow Jesus entry. God has given each one of us free will and He will never violate that free will of choice to accept or reject him.

It is exactly the same way with demons. Demons cannot enter into a person unless a decision is made based on a free will choice that connects you with the demon. That decision then provides them legal access to our hearts.

This helps give more clarify to the scripture, **Proverbs 23:7** For as he thinketh in his heart, so is he....

If a person has negative thoughts about themselves; if those thoughts are not dealt with they can affect specific parts of the body that connect to the negative thoughts.

Eventually it could lead to a demonic influence affecting those specific parts of the body by expressing itself in a sickness or disease.

Example in the Bible:

And he was teaching in one of the synagogues on the Sabbath. And, behold, there was a woman who had a spirit of infirmity eighteen years, and was bowed together, and could in no wise lift up herself. And when Jesus saw her, he called her to him, and said unto her, Woman, thou art loosed from thine infirmity. And he laid his hands on her: and immediately she was made straight, and glorified God. **Luke 13:10 – 13**

She had a spirit of infirmity for eighteen years.

THE SECRET TO THE HEALING POWER

In the Greek spirit is defined as from G4154; a current of air, that is, breath (blast) or a breeze; by analogy or figuratively a spirit, that is, (human) the rational soul, (by implication) vital principle, mental disposition, etc., or (superhuman) an angel, demon, or (divine) God, Christ's spirit, the Holy spirit: – ghost, life, spirit (-ual, - ually), mind. In this case a demon had affected her body and bound her with some type of disease or infirmity.

In the Greek, infirmity is defined as feebleness (of body or mind); by implication malady; moral frailty: – disease, infirmity, sickness, weakness.

The bible does not indicate what had opened the door for the spirit of infirmity. But based on the weakness of the body we could possibly consider:

- **Unconfessed sin in one's life**
  But let a man examine himself, and so let him eat of that bread, and drink of that cup. For he that eateth and drinketh unworthily, eateth and drinketh damnation to himself, not discerning the Lord's body. For this cause many are weak and sickly among you, and many sleep. **1 Corinthians 11:28, 30**
- **Hereditary weakness or disease, and words from our mouth** that speaks of infirmity or confession of a infirmity – "I think I have cancer or some type of disease or I have what my family has." For as he thinketh in his heart, so is he: **Proverb 23:7**
- **Not taking care of your health or body or a desire to be sick for various illogical reasons.**
  Beloved, I wish above all things that thou mayest prosper and be in health, even as thy soul prospereth. **III John 1:2**
  What? know ye not that your body is the temple of the Holy Ghost which is in you, which ye have of God, and ye are not your own? For ye are bought with a price: therefore glorify God in your body, and in your spirit, which are God's. **I Corinthians 6: 19 – 20**

Once we agree with the enemy regarding any thought, idea, negative feelings or action(s), we give the devil legal right into our lives. He will then begin to manifest or express in sickness, disease, circumstances, finances, etc.

Negative events are not always related to the demonic but if we don't address the issues of our hearts and thought life there is potential for the demonic to come into our lives if we allow legal access by agreement.

Chapter 9
The Power of Forgiveness

My wife and I were invited to a meeting with a man of God named Apostle Tony Kemp. As he began to minister in the Word of God, he talked about forgiveness. We know that Jesus Christ forgave us for our sins on the cross. Through faith in Jesus and repentance, we have been brought to a place of fellowship with the Father through Jesus.

I had never related forgiveness and repentance to healing. Apostle Kemp told the congregation about a young lady who was a preacher who contracted cancer in her body and blindness in one of her eyes. When she was a little girl, about 8 years old, she and her friend were crossing the street. She crossed the street first and turned around and beckoned to her friend to cross the street. As the friend began to cross the street the driver of a car didn't see her and struck her. The little girl died that day. The death of her friend devastated the young woman at the age of eight and she blamed herself for her death. Over the years as she got older the self-guilt that was planted in her heart began to manifest in cancer and her body began to eat itself away. The main eye that had witnessed the accident became self-destructive and she lost her sight in that eye. The manifested nature of the diseases took hold of her life and tried to destroy her. The disease used the self-guilt to consume her and the eye that saw the accident began to die.

Self-guilt can manifest because of unforgiveness and cause sickness and disease to gain legal access to the body.

As she was ministered to about the power of forgiveness, she forgave herself and the self-guilt left her body. Self-guilt no longer had a hold on her because she forgave herself. The disease that had invaded her body had no legitimate right to stay in her body so it had to leave. Immediately her blind eye was opened and the cancer in her body left. She was made whole by the power of God.

As I listened, I began to examine my heart and identified unforgiveness in my heart. It caused me to begin to pray, forgive others that had hurt me, forgive myself for my self-guilt and most of all I had to ask God to forgive me for blaming Him for things that had occurred in my life.

There is another powerful testimony from a preacher who had several problems with his body. He was born with a short leg, his back was out of alignment, and he also had a problem with his neck. He was in pain all his life. He recognized that he had unforgiveness toward his mother and also against himself.

He talked about how when his mother was pregnant with him she tried to abort him. The doctor was unable to abort him because of his position in the womb. He felt rejected by his mother and he also rejected himself because of the physical condition of his body.

The revelation of the Word of God about forgiveness immediately changed him and he forgave his mother and himself. Jesus touched him and immediately his leg grew by 3 inches, the bones in his back that were out of alignment moved into their proper position and the pain in his neck left. He was completely healed.

THE SECRET TO THE HEALING POWER

Forgiveness and repentance is tied to your thinking and emotions. The Word of God indicates, "as a man thinketh in his heart, so is he."

Whatever thought is in our minds, that is what we shall manifest, whether negative or positive. We reflect the character and attributes of our way of thinking. Your body can react and conform to how you think.

Chapter 10
How to Receive your Healing

To receive your healing, you must ensure that:

- You are living the life of the Scriptures through faith
- You have faith in the Word of God concerning healing
- All doubts and tares are removed
- You confess the Word of faith regarding the area of sickness or disease.
- You duplicate God's pattern of speaking
- You eat the proper foods
- You exercise the body
- You begin thanking God for His provision of healing

God's Redemption Plan Includes Healing:

Isaiah 53:5 But he was wounded for our transgressions, he was bruised for our iniquities: the chastisement of our peace was upon him; and with his stripes we are healed.

He was wounded for our transgressions – healed or mended from a broken relationship

He was bruised for our iniquities – healed from the effects of iniquity – ways of thinking/living

The chastisement of our peace was upon him – judgment is removed

By His stripes we are healed – complete healing in body, soul and spirit

There are Three Types of Healing Identified in the Bible.

Category One

Sozo (Strong's number is G4982) Salvation – restoring spirit, soul and body

Category Two

Therapeuo (G2323 and G2322)

Therapeutic – To cure through various ways God provides "Gifts of Healings"

Category Three

Iaomai (G2390) and **Iama** (G2386) One way of healing Instantaneous miraculous healing

Example – identify in the Bible

Act 28:8 And it came to pass, that the father of Publius lay sick of a fever and of a bloody flux: to whom Paul entered in, and prayed, and laid his hands on him, and healed him. (Iaomai G2590 – Instantaneous)

Act 28:9 So when this was done, others also, which had diseases in the island, came, and were healed: (Therapeuo – G2525 and G2522 – Gradual Healing)

When we find out that there is sickness or disease in our bodies, ***"Never Claim It"*** – don't say words like "I have" or "they said I have". What you say is what you can have because you claim healing, it is yours. You can give legal right to the sickness and/or disease by what you declare.

This is not to say you don't have the symptoms, pain, sickness disease or etc. But declaring these, you allow <u>legal access to your body.</u> Think of it as a thief coming into your house uninvited. The thief is there to try to steal what does not belong to him; health, peace and joy. When we say "I have this;" we are saying you can come in proceed to take what does not belong to him.

Once the thief is in the house, you must defend it with weapons or whatever you have; or you can help him carry your stuff out of your house by saying "you want my health, peace or joy – I will give it to you – I will help you carry it out of my house." ***<u>DON'T DO IT!</u>***

The following Scriptures will help you set your foundation for receiving and maintaining your healing and health.

Put in memory the following Scriptural principles:

Luke 1:37 – For no word from God shall be void of power. ASV ***(Every Word from God is full of Power)***

Isaiah 55:11 – So shall my word be that goeth forth out of my mouth: it shall not return unto me void, but it shall accomplish that which I please, and it shall prosper in the thing whereto I sent it.

There two things about God that is impossible:

God cannot lie and cannot change (**Hebrew 6:18**) That by two immutable things, in which it was impossible for God to lie, we might have a strong consolation, who have fled for refuge to lay hold upon the hope set before us:

Exodus 23:25 And ye shall serve the LORD your God, and he shall bless thy bread, and thy water; and I will take sickness away from the midst of thee.

Exodus 23:26 There shall nothing cast their young, nor be barren, in thy land: the number of thy days I will fulfil.

These are foundational steps you can take to start the process. Remember, God can heal you anyway He wants so give Him the freedom to do so.

Step 1 – Identify the illness, sickness or disease in the body and what part of the body.

Example: arm, leg(s) or weakness in the body, etc. What is the diagnosis from the doctor?

- When did the symptoms first appear or manifest?
- What is the characteristic of the illness, sickness or disease?

These are necessary to speak to the illness, sickness or disease.

Step 2 – Do you know the source of the illness, sickness or disease?

If not, ask the Holy Spirit to reveal it to you during your prayer time.

Remember the following are sources that illness, sickness or disease come from:

- **Generational Curses** – Passed down from one generation to another
- **Natural Environment** – Substances in the air
- **Natural decline of the human body** – Age (Curse of Adam)
- **Emotions which cause stress** (Trauma, etc.)
- **One's Mindset** – How a person thinks about oneself
- **Demons** – May be result of sin (oppression/legal right)

Knowing the source helps to understand how to pray and deal with the source and close the door to it.

Step 3 – Examination of the Heart

Begin to pray and examine your heart and ask God through His Holy Spirit in Jesus' Name to reveal anything that you may have in your heart:

- Sin
- Unconfessed sins
- Repentance from your sins
- Forgiving others and forgiving yourself and your body. Sometimes we talk against our bodies if they don't function correctly.
- Ask God to forgive you for blaming Him

Matthews 5:8 Blessed are the pure in heart: for they shall see God.

The Greek word for Pure is defined as G2513 kath-ar-os. Of uncertain affinity; clean (literally or figuratively): – clean, clear, pure. It is identified with the process of cleaning. Examine and remove the stain to make one's heart pure.

1 John 1:8 If we say that we have no sin, we deceive ourselves, and the truth is not in us.

1 John 1:9 If we confess our sins, he is faithful and just to forgive us our sins, and to cleanse us from all unrighteousness.

Step 4 – Meditate on and confess healing Scripture

Everyday meditate on and confess the Word of God pertaining to your illness until you experience the healing and restoring Power of God.

Psalms 1:2 But his delight is in the law of the LORD; and in his law doth he meditate day and night.

Psalms 1:3 And he shall be like a tree planted by the rivers of water, that bringeth forth his fruit in his season; his leaf also shall not wither; and whatsoever he doeth shall prosper.

Joshua 1:8 This book of the law shall not depart out of thy mouth; but thou shalt meditate therein day and night, that thou mayest observe to do according to all that is written therein: for then thou shalt make thy way prosperous, and then thou shalt have good success.

Psalms 107:20 He sent his word, and healed them, and delivered them from their destructions.

Proverbs 4:20 – 22 My son, attend to my words; incline thine ear unto my sayings. Let them not depart from thine eyes; keep them in the midst of thine heart. For they are life unto those that find them, and health to all their flesh.

Find specific Bible scripture(s) that address the issue. *(See the section "Healing Scriptures for Specific Body Parts".)*

Example:

Problems with your Bones Scriptures Regarding Bone problems:

- **Proverbs 3:8** It shall be health to thy navel, and marrow to thy bones.
- **Isaiah 58:11** And the LORD shall guide thee continually, and satisfy thy soul in drought, and make fat thy bones: and thou shalt be like a watered garden, and like a spring of water, whose waters fail not.
- **Psalms 34:19** Many are the afflictions of the righteous: but the LORD delivereth him out of them all.
- **Psalms 34:20** He keepeth all his bones: not one of them is broken.

Step 5 – Eat Healthy Food

Begin to eat food that helps the area of your body that is being affected. Add fasting and prayer daily, a couple of hours a day. Rest and exercise your body. Follow your doctor's orders and diet plan.

Step 6 – Faith

Keep the switch of Faith on and stay away from negative words and people. Once healed, provide a testimony to Glory of God

Disclaimer, God can heal anybody anyway He wants. The following are other ways God can provide healing. Always be open to the Healing power of God. *GOD CAN DO ANYTHING BUT FAIL!!*

Chapter 11
Meditate on the Word of God

Meditating on the Word of God has everything to do with seeing or viewing what God is speaking. The definition of meditating in Hebrew is hâgâh (H1897) 'haw-gaw' to ponder, imagine, meditate, mourn, mutter, roar, speak, study, talk, utter.

King James Concordance – Total KJV Occurrences of H1897: 24, which are translated as: meditate, 6 (Jos_1:8, Psa_1:2, Psa_63:6, Psa_77:12, Psa_143:5, Isa_33:18), mourn, 4 (Isa_16:7, Isa_38:14, Isa_59:11, Jer_48:31), speak, 3 (Psa_35:28, Pro_8:7 (2)), imagine, 2 (Psa_2:1, Psa_38:12, studieth, 2 (Pro_15:28, Pro_24:2), mutter, 1 (Isa_8:19), muttered, 1 (Isa_59:3), roaring, 1 (Isa_31:3-4 (2)), speaketh, 1 (Psa_37:30), talk, 1 (Psa_71:24), utter, 1 (Job_27:4), uttering, 1 (Isa_59:1

As you read the definition, what you find is meditation is about imagining what is being said or what you read in the scriptures. The scriptures are God's Word to mankind regarding the issues and concerns of life. The Scriptures give directions to be complete in spirit, soul, and body. Jesus speaks about the characteristics of His Word. His Word is living and active. It is ready to manifest what it is speaking.

It is the spirit that quickeneth; the flesh profiteth nothing: the words that I speak unto you, "they are spirit, and they are life". **John 6:63**

So shall my word be that goeth forth out of my mouth: it shall not return unto me void, but it shall accomplish that which I please, and it shall prosper in the thing whereto I sent it. **Isaiah 55:11**

Then said the LORD unto me, Thou hast well seen: for I will hasten my word to perform it. **Jeremiah 1:12**

God's Word has the power to perform or bring to pass God's purpose and promises for your life.

Because the Word of God is the foundation from which everything was made, it is natural to understand that if the Word created it, it also can correct any problem that may occur.

If there are sicknesses in the body as a result of a germ or virus, it is the Word's job to correct the problem. This is where meditating on the Word of God come in.

Meditating on the Word through faith that deals with the problem allows the Word of God to take action against the germ or virus. The following are the steps that bring the Word of God into action.

The scripture that deals with the problem requires meditating on that Word until it becomes a reality in your heart and mind. I believe it because faith comes by hearing and hearing by the Word of God.

Meditate on that Word until you can see the reality of the Word in your heart and mind. It must become a reality in your heart and mind through your imagination.

Once you have faith in the Word and meditate on it until it become a reality in your heart and mind, the Word of God will become living/alive.

THE SECRET TO THE HEALING POWER

Once it becomes living in your heart and mind, the Word become full of Power to overcome sickness or virus.

Meditation is a key to unlock the supernatural aspect of God.

Isaiah 66:2 For all those things hath mine hand made, and all those things have been, saith the LORD: but to this man will I look, even to him that is poor and of a contrite spirit, and trembleth at my word.

Jermiah 23:28 The prophet that hath a dream, let him tell a dream; and he that hath my word, let him speak my word faithfully. What is the chaff to the wheat? saith the LORD.

Jermiah 23:29 Is not my word like as a fire? saith the LORD; and like a hammer that breaketh the rock in pieces?

St John 5:24 Verily, verily, I say unto you, He that heareth my word, and believeth on him that sent me, hath everlasting life, and shall not come into condemnation; but is passed from death unto life.

Chapter 12
Emotional Causes of Disease

Emotional Causes of Disease Starting with A

ABDOMINAL CRAMPS: Fear, stopping the process. The inability to keep at something.

ABSCESS: Fermenting thoughts over hurts, such as neglect, and jealousy, slights, and revenge.

ACCIDENTS: Inability to speak up for oneself; always being sidelined, overlooked, or exploited because of the inability to speak up. Rebellion against authority. Belief in violence.

ACHES: Longing for love. Longing to be held. Emotional neediness

ACNE: Not accepting or disliking oneself. Low self-esteem and value for oneself.

ADENOIDS: Family friction, arguments. A child who feels unwelcome due to the existence of a defective ego.

THE SECRET TO THE HEALING POWER

ADDICTIONS: Running away from self, not facing fear. Not knowing how to love oneself.

ADDISON'S DISEASE: Severe emotional malnutrition. Anger at self; stems from rejection and past hurts.

ADRENAL PROBLEMS: Defeatism; lacking value for one's needs. No longer caring for oneself, anxiety.

AGING PROBLEMS: Social beliefs. Old thinking. Fear of being oneself. Rejection of the now.

ALCOHOLISM/ABUSE: Futility, guilt, inadequacy, self-rejection

ALLERGY AND HAYFEVER: You are allergic to someone (or yourself) who denies your power. Irritated by life.

ALZHEIMER'S DISEASE: Desire to leave the planet. The inability to face life as it is.

AMNESIA: Fear. Running from life. Inability to stand up for oneself.

ANEMIA: Yes-but attitude. Lack of joy. Fear of life. Feeling not good enough.

ANKLE PROBLEMS: Inflexibility and guilt. Inability to receive pleasure. Represent mobility and direction

ANORECTAL BLEEDING: Anger and frustration.

ANOREXIA: Denying oneself and life. Extreme fear of rejection.

ANUS: Releasing point. Dumping ground.

ANUS/ABSCESS: Anger concerning what you don't want to release.

ANAL BLEEDING: (See ANORECTAL Bleeding)

ANUS, FISTULA: Incomplete releasing of trash. Holding on to garbage of the past. Unforgiveness; self-imprisonment of soul.

ANUS, ITCHING: Guilt over the past, metaphysical restriction of our minds. Remorse.

ANUS PAIN: Guilt. The desire for punishment. Not good enough.

ANXIETY/NERVOUSNESS: Distrust of the natural flow and process of life.

APATHY: Resistance to feeling. Deadening of the self. Fear.

APPENDICITIS: Fear. Fear of life. Blocking the flow of good.

APPETITE, EXCESSIVE: Fear. Needing protection. Judging the emotions.

APPETITE, LOSS OF: Fear. Protecting the self. Distrusting life.

ARM PROBLEMS: Represents the capacity and ability to hold the experience of life.

ARTERIOSCLEROSIS: RESISTANCE, tension. Hardened and narrow-mindedness. Refusing to see good.

ARTERIES: Carry the joy of life.

ARTHRITIS: Feeling unloved, criticism, resentment, bitterness. Feeling not good enough.

ARTHRITIC FINGERS: A desire to punish. Blame. Feeling victimized.

ASPHYXIATING ATTACKS: Fear. Distrusting life. Stuck in childhood.

ASTHMA: Unresolved guilt. Smothering love. Inability to breathe for oneself. Feeling stifled. Suppressed crying.

ATHLETE'S FOOT: Frustration at not being accepted. Inability to move forward with ease.

Emotional Causes of Disease Starting with B

BACKS: Represent the support of life.

BACK PROBLEMS:

UPPER: Lack of emotional support or feeling unloved.

MIDDLE: Guilt. Being stuck in all the guilt of the past stuffed back there or get-off-my-back feelings.

LOWER: Financial woes and concerns. Fear of money. Lack of financial support.

BABY ASTHMA: Fear of life. Not wanting to be here.

BAD BREATH: The thought of anger and revenge. Experiences backing up.

BALANCE, LOSS OF: Scattered thinking. Not centered.

BALDNESS: Fear, tension. Trying to control everything and not trusting in the process of life.

BED-WETTING: Fear of parents. Usually, father

BELCHING: Fear, gulping life too quickly.

BIRTH DEFECTS: Karmic. You selected to come out that way. We choose our parents.

BLACKHEADS (PIMPLES): Feeling dirty and unloved

BLADDER PROBLEMS: Anxiety. Holding on to old ideas. Fear of letting go. Being pissed off.

BLEEDING: Joy running out. Anger, but where?

BLEEDING GUMS: Lack of joy in the decisions made in life.

BLISTERS: Resistance. Lack of emotional protection.

BLOOD: Represents joy in the body, flowing freely.

BLOOD PROBLEMS: Lack of joy. Lack of circulation ideas.

ANEMIC: (SEE ANAEMIA)

BLOOD CLOTTING: Closing down the flow of joy.

BLOOD PRESSURE:

>**HIGH (Hypertension):** Longstanding emotional problems not solved. (Possibility generational)
>
>**LOW:** Lack of love as a child. Defeatism. "What's the use? It won't work anyway."

BODY ODOR: Fear. Dislike of the self. Fear of others.

BOILS: Anger, boiling over. Seething.

BONES: Represent the structure of the universe.

BONE PROBLEMS:

BREAKS: Rebelling against authority.

DEFORMITY: Mental pressure and tightness. Muscles can't stretch. Loss of mental mobility.

BOWEL: Represents the release of waste. Fear of letting go of the old and no longer needed.

BRAIN: Represents the computer, the switchboard.

TUMOR: Incorrect computerized beliefs. Stubborn. Refusing to change the old patterns.

BREAST: Represents mothering and nurturing.

> **BREAST (left):** Feeling unloved, refusing to nourish oneself. Putting everyone else first.

> **BREAST (right):** Over-protection, overbearing, difficulty in giving love.

BREAST PROBLEMS –Cysts, lumps, soreness: over-mothering, overprotection, overbearing attitudes. Cutting off nourishment.

BREATH: Represents the ability to take in life.

BREATHING PROBLEMS: Fear or the refusal to take in life. Not feeling worthy to take up space.

BRIGHT'S DISEASE: Feeling like a kid who can't do it right and isn't good enough. A failure. Loss.

BRONCHITIS: Inflamed family environment. Arguments and yelling. Rarely silent.

BRUISES: Self-punishment.

BULIMIA: Hopeless terror. Purging self-hatred.

BURNS: Anger, burning up inside.

BURSITIS: Repressed anger. Wanting to hit someone.

BUTTOCKS: Represents power. Loose buttocks, loss of power.

Emotional Causes of Disease Starting with C

CALLUSES: Hardened concepts and Ideas. Fear solidified.

CANKER SORES: Festering words held back by the lips. Blame

CANCER: What's eating at you? Deep hurt, secret, or grief. Long-standing resentment.

CARBUNCLE: Poisonous anger about personal injustices.

CAR-SICKNESS: Fear. Bondage. Feeling of being trapped.

CARPAL TUNNEL: Anger and frustrations at life's seeming injustices.

CATARACTS: Inability to see ahead with joy. Dark future.

CHILDHOOD DISEASES: Belief in calendars, social concepts, and false laws. Childish behavior in the adults around them.

CHILLS: Mental contraction. Pulling away and into something. Desire to retreat

CHRONIC DISEASES: A refusal to change. Fear of the future. Not feeling safe.

CHOLESTEROL (high): Clogging the channels of joy.

CIRCULATION: Lack of joy or the lack of circulation of ideas.

COLDS: Too much going on at once. Mental confusion and disorder.

COLD SORES: Festering angry words and fear of expressing them.

COLIC: Mental irritation. Annoyance with surroundings.

COLITIS: Over-exacting parents. Feeling of oppression and defeat. Great need for affection.

COMA: Fear. Trying to escape from something or someone.

CONJUNCTIVITIS: Anger and frustration at what you are looking in life.

CONSTIPATION: Refusing to release old ideas

CORONARY THROMBOSIS: Feeling alone and scared. Not good enough. Don't do enough. Will never make it.

COUGHS: A desire to bark at the world. "Listen to me!"

CRAMPS: Tension. Fear. Gripping. Holding on.

CROUP: (SEE BRONCHITIS)

CRYING: Tears are the river of life. Shed in joy as well as sadness and fear.

CUSHING'S DISEASE: Mental imbalance. Overproduction of crushing ideas. A feeling of being overpowered

CUTS: Punishment for not following your own rules.

CYSTS: Running the old painful movie. Nursing hurts. A false growth.

CYSTIC FIBROSIS: A thick belief that life won't work for you. Poor me.

Emotional Causes of Disease Starting with D

DEPRESSION: Anger, hopelessness.

DIABETES: Longing for what might have been. No sweetness left in life.

DIARRHEA: Fear and rejection. Running off or away from something or someone.

DIZZINESS: Flighty, scattered thinking.

Emotional Causes of Disease Starting with E

EAR PROBLEMS: Not wanting to hear. Anger or too much turmoil

ELBOW PROBLEMS: Not being flexible, not able to change directions or accept new experiences.

EYE PROBLEMS: (Children): Not wanting to see what's going on in the family.

    EYE (astigmatism): Fear of "seeing" the self.

    EYES (cataracts): Inability to see ahead with joy.

    EYE (Farsighted): Fear of the present.

    EYE (Nearsighted): Fear of the future.

    EYE STY: Looking at life through angry eyes. Being angry at someone.

Emotional Causes of Disease Starting with F

FAINTING: Fear, can't cope, inability to survive, blocking out what's really going on.

FEET PROBLEMS: Fear of the future or not wanting to move forward.

FEMALE PROBLEMS: Denial of the self and rejecting the feminine aspects within.

FEVERS and INFECTIONS: Anger, burning up.

FIBROIDS: Nursing a hurt from a partner, a blow to the feminine ego

FINGER (thumb): Worry, always thinking. Being 'under someone's thumb'.

FINGER (index): Fear of authority, or egotistical; abusing your authority.

FLU: Responding to mass negativity. Putting too much faith in statistics.

Emotional Causes of Diseases Starting with G

GAS PAIN (flatulence): Undigested ideas or concerns.

GRAY HAIR: Stress, feeling under pressure and strain.

GUM PROBLEMS: Inability to back up decisions. Being wishy-washy about life.

Emotional Causes of Diseases Starting with H

HAND PROBLEMS: Grasping on too tight, not wanting to let go. Not 'handling' things well.

HEADACHE: Self-criticism. Not wanting to accept what is going on.

HEART ATTACK: Squeezing all the joy out of life, in favor of money or position.

HEARTBURN (acid reflux): Clutching onto fear. Not trusting in the process of life.

HEART PROBLEMS: Lack of joy, dealing with issues from anger, not love.

HEMORRHOIDS: Fear of deadlines. Afraid to let go and move on.

HERNIA: Ruptured relationships, feeling burdens.

HIP PROBLEMS: Fear of going forward in major decisions.

HIVES (rash or Urticaria): Small, hidden fears. Mountains out of molehills.

HYPERACTIVITY: Feeling pressured and frantic.

HYPERVENTILATION: Resisting change. Not being able to take it all in.

Emotional Causes of Diseases Starting with I

IMPOTENCE: Sexual guilt or pressure, feeling spite against a previous mate.

INDIGESTION: Dread or anxiety about a recent or coming event.

INFECTION: Irritation, anger, or annoyance about a recent situation.

INSOMNIA: It is associated with feelings of fear and guilt and not trusting the process of life. Anxiety issues.

Emotional Causes of Diseases Starting with K

KIDNEY PROBLEMS: Criticism, disappointment, failure. Shame. Reacting like a little kid.

    KIDNEY STONES: Lumps of unresolved anger.

KNEE PROBLEMS: Stubborn ego and pride. Inability to bend. Inflexibility. Won't give in.

Emotional Causes of Diseases Starting with L

LARYNGITIS: Fear of speaking up.

LEFT SIDE OF BODY: The feminine side. Represents receptivity, taking in, women, mothers, and love.

LEG PROBLEMS: Fear of the future, not being able to carry things forward.

LIVER PROBLEMS (hepatitis): Resistance to change. Fear, anger, and hatred. The liver is the seat of anger and rage.

LUNG PROBLEMS: Depression, grief, or fear of life. Not feeling worthy.

LUPUS: A giving up. Better to die than stand up for oneself. Anger and punishment.

Emotional Causes of Diseases Starting with M

MENOPAUSE: Fear of no longer being wanted.

MENTAL ALERTNESS and SENILITY: Returning to the "safety" of childhood. Demanding care and attention.

MIGRAINE HEADACHE: Sexual fears, or fear of being close, letting someone in too close. Feeling driven or pressured.

MENSTRUAL IMBALANCE/PMS: Rejection of one's femininity. Guilt or feeling "dirty".

Emotional Causes of Diseases Starting with N

NAUSEA: Fear, rejecting an idea or experience.

NECK PROBLEMS: Refusing to see another's side or position. Stubbornness. Who or what is being a pain in the neck?

Emotional Causes of Diseases Starting with O

OSTEOPOROSIS: Feeling there is no support left in life.

OVERWEIGHT: Fear, feeling a deep need for emotional protection. Running away from feelings, insecurity, over sensitivity. Often represents fear and shows a need for protection. Fear may be a cover for hidden anger and a resistance to forgiving. Running away from feelings. Insecurity, self-rejection, and seeking fulfillment.

Weight issues in certain areas of the body:

- Arms: Anger at being denied, love.
- Belly: Anger at being denied nourishment.
- Hips: Lumps of stubborn anger at the parents.
- Thighs: Packed childhood anger. Often rage at the father.

Emotional Causes of Diseases Starting with P

PAIN: Self-punishment, feeling emotional guilt.

PANCREAS: Represents the sweetness of life.

PANCREATITIS: Rejection. Anger and frustration because life seems to have lost its sweetness.

PARALYSIS: Fear, terror. Escaping a situation or a person. Resistance.

PARKINSON'S DISEASE: Fear and intense desire to control everything and everyone.

PEPTIC ULCER: Fear. A belief that you are not good enough. Anxious to please.

PHLEBITIS: Anger and frustration. Blaming others for the limitation and lack of joy in life.

PILES: See Hemorrhoids.

PETIT MAL: See Epilepsy.

PINK EYE: Anger and frustration. Not wanting to see.

PITUITARY GLAND: Represents the control center.

PLANTAR WART: Anger at the very basis of your understanding. Spreading frustration about the future.

PNEUMONIA: Desperate. Tired of life. Emotional wounds that are not allowed to heal.

POLIO: Paralyzing jealousy. A desire to stop someone.

POST NASAL DRIP: Inner crying. Childish tears. Victim.

(P.M.S) PREMENSTRUAL SYNDROME: Allowing confusion to reign. Giving power to outside influences. Rejection of the feminine processes.

PSORIASIS: Fear of being hurt. Deadening the senses and the senses. Refusing to accept responsibility for our feelings.

PROSTRATE: Represents the masculine principle.

PROSTATE PROBLEMS: Mental fears weakening masculinity. Sexual pressure and feelings of guilt or inadequacy.

PUBIC BONE: Represents protection.

PUBIC HAIR: Represents both attraction and hiding. Neither children nor the elderly have pubic hair.

PYORRHOEA: Anger at the inability to make decisions. Wishy-washy people.

Emotional Causes of Diseases Starting with Q

QUINSY: A strong belief that you cannot speak up for yourself and ask for your needs.

Emotional Causes of Diseases Starting with R

RABIES: Anger. A belief that violence is the answer.

RECTUM: See Anus.

RASH: Irritation over delays. A babyish way to get attention.

RESPIRATORY AILMENTS: Fear of taking in life fully.

RHEUMATISM: Feeling victimized. Lack of love. Chronic bitterness. Resentment.

RHEUMATOID ARTHRITIS: Deep criticism of authority. Feeling very put upon.

RICKETS: Emotional malnutrition. Lack of love and security.

RIGHT SIDE OF BODY: Giving out, letting go, masculine energy, men, the father.

RINGWORM: Allowing others to get under your skin. Not feeling good enough or clean enough.

ROUND SHOULDERS: Carrying the burdens of life. Helpless and hopeless.

Emotional Causes of Diseases Starting with S

SAGGING LINES: Sagging lines on the face comes from sagging thoughts in the mind. Resentment of life.

SCABIES: Infected thinking. Allowing others to get under your skin.

SCIATICA: Being hypocritical. Fear of money and of the future.

SCOLIOSIS: See round shoulders

SCRATCHES: Feeling life tears at you, that life is a rip-off.

SEA SICKNESS: Fear. Fear of Death. Lack of control.

SENILITY: Returning to the so-called safety of childhood. Demanding care and attention. A form of control over those around you. Escapism.

SICKLE CELL ANEMIA: A belief that one is not good enough that destroys the very joy of life.

SEIZURES: Running away from the self, family, or life.

SHOULDERS: Are meant to carry joy, not burdens.

   SHOULDER PROBLEMS: Carrying the weight of the world on your shoulders. Feeling like life is a burden.

SHINGLES: Waiting for the other shoe to drop. Fear and tension. Too sensitive.

SINUS PROBLEMS: Irritation with someone, usually someone close to you.

SKIN: Protects our individuality. A sense organ.

SKIN CONDITIONS: Anxiety, fear, feeling threatened. Old buried gunk.

SLIPPED DISK: Feeling unsupported in life.

SOLAR PLEXUS: Ignoring 'gut instincts or your intuitions.

SORE THROAT: Holding in angry words. Feeling unable to express oneself.

SNORING: Stubborn refusal to let go of old patterns.

SPASMS: I release all restrictions, and I am free to be me.

SPINE: Flexible support of life.

SPINAL CURVATURE: The inability to flow with the support of life. Fear and trying to hold onto new ideas. Distrusting life. Lack of integrity. No courage of convictions.

SPLEEN PROBLEMS: Obsessions. Being obsessed about things.

SPRAINS: Anger and resistance. Not wanting to move in a certain direction in life.

STERILITY: Fear and resistance to the process of life. Not needing to go through the parenting experience.

STIFFNESS: Rigid, stiff thinking.

STIFF NECK: Un-bending bull-headedness

STOMACH: Holds nourishment. Digest ideas and feelings.

   STOMACH and INTESTINAL PROBLEMS: Dread, fear of the new, or not feeling nourished.

STROKE: Insecurity, lack of self-expression. Not being allowed to cry.

STUTTERING: Insecurity. Lack of expression. Not being allowed to cry.

SWELLING: Being stuck in thinking. Clogged, painful ideas.

SYPHILIS: (SEE VENEREAL DISEASE)

Emotional Causes of Diseases Starting with T

TAPEWORM: Strong belief in being a victim and unclean. Helpless to the seeming attitudes of others.

TETANUS: A need to release angry festering thoughts.

TEETH PROBLEMS: Being indecisive, not being able to break down ideas for analysis and decisions.

TINNITUS: Refusal to listen. Not hearing the inner voice. Stubbornness.

TESTICULAR PROBLEMS: Not accepting masculine principles, or masculinity within.

THROAT: Avenue of expression. Channel of creativity.

THROAT PROBLEMS: The inability to speak up for oneself. Swallowed anger. Stifled creativity. Refusal to change

THRUSH (VAGINAL INFECTION): Feeling sexually abused or exploited. Feelings of guilt, shame or repressed sexual feelings, or being intimate with the wrong person.

THYROID PROBLEMS: Humiliation. Feeling repressed or put down. Feeling as if you never get to do what you want.

TONSILLITIS: Fear. Repressed emotions. Stifled creativity.

TOES: Represents the minor details of the future.

TUBERCULOSIS: Wasting away from selfishness. Possessive, or cruel thoughts. Revenge

TUMORS: Nursing old hurts and shocks. Building on remorse.

Emotional Causes of Diseases Starting with U

ULCERS: Fear, a strong belief that you are not good enough. "What is eating away at you?"

URINARY PROBLEMS: Feeling pissed off! Usually at the opposite sex or lover.

UTERUS: Represents the home of creativity.

Emotional Causes of Diseases Starting with V

VAGINITIS: Anger at a mate. Sexual guilt. Punishing the self.

VARICOSE VEINS: Standing in a situation you hate. Feeling overworked and overburdened.

VENEREAL DISEASE: Sexual guilt. Need for punishment. Believe that the genitals are sinful or dirty.

VERTIGO: Flighty, Scattered thinking. A refusal to look.

VITILIGO: Not belonging. Feeling completely outside of things. Not one of the groups.

VULVA: Represents vulnerability.

Emotional Causes of Diseases Starting with W

WARTS: Little expression of hate. One's belief in ugliness.

WISDOM TOOTH IMPACTED: Not giving mental space to create a firm foundation.

WRIST: Represents movements and ease.

Chapter 13
God's Methods of Healing

There are many methods by which God heals. The most powerful and effective method is the Word itself. Here is a list of some other methods God uses:

- **The spoken Word** – Isaiah 53:4, Matthew 8:17, I Peter 2:24, Psalm 107:20, Luke 7:1-10
- **The laying on of hands** – Matthew 20:34, Mark 1:41, 6:5, 7:33, 8:22-25, Luke 4:40, 13:13, 20:50,51, Acts 9:10-12, 17, 28:8, James 5:11.
- **The anointing of oil and prayer of faith** – James 5:14,15, Exodus 40:9-11, 28:41, Mark 11:24.
- **Gifts of the Holy Spirit** – Act 3:2-6, I Corinthians 12:9-10, 30.
- **The name of Jesus Christ** – Act 3:1-7, Philip 2:9, Ephesians 1:21
- **Apron and handkerchief** – Act 19:11-12
- **Angels** – St.John 5:4
- **Realm of Glory** – Psalm 105:37
- **Doctors** – 2 Kings 20:7 Matthew 9:12

Chapter 14
Healing Scriptures for Specific Body Parts

ABDOMEN

Proverbs 3:8 It shall be health to thy navel, and marrow to thy bones.

Proverbs 18:20 A man's belly shall be satisfied with the fruit of his mouth; and with the increase of his lips shall he be filled.

Song of Solomon 7:2 Thy navel is like a round goblet, which wanteth not liquor: thy belly is like a heap of wheat set about with lilies.

Deuteronomy 28:27 The LORD will smite thee with the botch of Egypt, and with the emerods, and with the scab, and with the itch, whereof thou canst not be healed.

Galatians 3:13 Christ hath redeemed us from the curse of the law, being made a curse for us: for it is written, Cursed is every one that hangeth on a tree:

Act 28:8 And it came to pass, that the father of Publius lay sick of a fever and of a bloody flux: to whom Paul entered in, and prayed, and laid his hands on him, and healed him.

Act 28:9 So when this was done, others also, which had diseases in the island, came, and were healed:

ANKLES - see: Feet/Joints

BACK

Psalms 145:14 The LORD upholdeth all that fall, and raiseth up all those that be bowed down.

Leviticus 21:18 For whatsoever man he be that hath a blemish, he shall not approach: a blind man, or a lame, or he that hath a flat nose, or anything superfluous,

Leviticus 21:20 Or crookback, or a dwarf, or that hath a blemish in his eye, or be scurvy, or scabbed, or hath his stones broken;

Leviticus 21:23 Only he shall not go in unto the vail, nor come nigh unto the altar, because he hath a blemish; that he profane not my sanctuaries: for I the LORD do sanctify them.

Luke 13:11 And, behold, there was a woman which had a spirit of infirmity eighteen years, and was bowed together, and could in no wise lift up herself.

Luke 13:13 And he laid his hands on her: and immediately she was made straight, and glorified God.

Luke 13:16 And ought not this woman, being a daughter of Abraham, whom Satan hath bound, lo, these eighteen years, be loosed from this bond on the sabbath day?

See also: Neck/Bones

BLOOD

Joe 3:21 For I will cleanse their blood that I have not cleansed: for the LORD dwelleth in Zion.

Ezekiel 16:6 And when I passed by thee, and saw thee polluted in thine own blood, I said unto thee when thou wast in thy blood, Live; yea, I said unto thee when thou wast in thy blood, Live.

Mark 5:29 And straightway the fountain of her blood was dried up; and she felt in her body that she was healed of that plague.

See also: Immune system/Infection/Bones

BONES

Proverbs 3:8 It shall be health to thy navel, and marrow to thy bones.

Isaiah 58:11 And the LORD shall guide thee continually, and satisfy thy soul in drought, and make fat thy bones: and thou shalt be like a watered garden, and like a spring of water, whose waters fail not.

Psalms 34:19 Many are the afflictions of the righteous: but the LORD delivereth him out of them all.

Psalms 34:20 He keepeth all his bones: not one of them is broken.

Act 3:6 Then Peter said, Silver and gold have I none; but such as I have give I thee: In the name of Jesus Christ of Nazareth rise up and walk.

Act 3:7 And he took him by the right hand, and lifted him up: and immediately his feet and ankle bones received strength.

See also: Joints/Teeth/Blood

BRAIN - see: Nervous system/Mental Health/Memory

BREAST - see: Reproductive system/Cancer/Tumors

BREATH - see: Respiratory system

COMPLEXION - see: Acne/Flesh/Skin

DIGESTION

Psalms 22:26 The meek shall eat and be satisfied: they shall praise the LORD that seek him: your heart shall live forever.

Mark 16:18 They shall take up serpents; and if they drink any deadly thing, it shall not hurt them; they shall lay hands on the sick, and they shall recover.

Matthew 15:17 Do not ye yet understand, that whatsoever entereth in at the mouth goeth into the belly, and is cast out into the draught?

Ecclesiastes 3:13 And also that every man should eat and drink, and enjoy the good of all his labour, it is the gift of God.

See also: Abdomen/Poisoning/Malnutrition/ Diarrhea/ Mouth

EARS

Proverbs 20:12 The hearing ear, and the seeing eye, the LORD hath made even both of them.

Isaiah 35:5 Then the eyes of the blind shall be opened, and the ears of the deaf shall be unstopped.

Isaiah 29:18 And in that day shall the deaf hear the words of the book, and the eyes of the blind shall see out of obscurity, and out of darkness.

Isaiah 32:3 And the eyes of them that see shall not be dim, and the ears of them that hear shall hearken.

EYES

Proverbs 20:12 The hearing ear, and the seeing eye, the LORD hath made even both of them.

Psalms 146:8 The LORD openeth the eyes of the blind: the LORD raiseth them that are bowed down: the LORD loveth the righteous:

Isaiah 35:4 Say to them that are of a fearful heart, Be strong, fear not: behold, your God will come with vengeance, even God with a recompence; he will come and save you.

Isaiah 35:5 Then the eyes of the blind shall be opened, and the ears of the deaf shall be unstopped.

Isaiah 29:18 And in that day shall the deaf hear the words of the book, and the eyes of the blind shall see out of obscurity, and out of darkness.

Isaiah 32:3 And the eyes of them that see shall not be dim, and the ears of them that hear shall hearken.

Deuteronomy 34:7 And Moses was an hundred and twenty years old when he died: his eye was not dim, nor his natural force abated.

Matthew 13:16 But blessed are your eyes, for they see: and your ears, for they hear.

FEET

1 Samuel 2:9 He will keep the feet of his saints, and the wicked shall be silent in darkness; for by strength shall no man prevail.

Psalms 91:11 For he shall give his angels charge over thee, to keep thee in all thy ways.

Psalms 91:12 They shall bear thee up in their hands, lest thou dash thy foot against a stone.

Psalms 121:3 He will not suffer thy foot to be moved: he that keepeth thee will not slumber.

Proverbs 3:23 Then shalt thou walk in thy way safely, and thy foot shall not stumble.

Proverbs 3:26 For the LORD shall be thy confidence, and shall keep thy foot from being taken.

Act 3:7 And he took him by the right hand, and lifted him up: and immediately his feet and ankle bones received strength.

Act 14:8 And there sat a certain man at Lystra, impotent in his feet, being a cripple from his mother's womb, who never had walked:

Act 14:10 Said with a loud voice, Stand upright on thy feet. And he leaped and walked.

Habakkuk 3:19 The LORD God is my strength, and he will make my feet like hinds' feet, and he will make me to walk upon mine high places. To the chief singer on my stringed instruments.

See also: Knees/Legs/Edema

FLESH

Proverb 4:22 For they are life unto those that find them, and health to all their flesh.

Job 33:24 Then he is gracious unto him, and saith, Deliver him from going down to the pit: I have found a ransom.

Job 33:25 His flesh shall be fresher than a child's: he shall return to the days of his youth:

Ezekiel 37:6 And I will lay sinews upon you, and will bring up flesh upon you, and cover you with skin, and put breath in you, and ye shall live; and ye shall know that I am the LORD.

2 Corinthians 4:11 For we which live are always delivered unto death for Jesus' sake, that the life also of Jesus might be made manifest in our mortal flesh.

Daniel 1:15 And at the end of ten days their countenances appeared fairer and fatter in flesh than all the children which did eat the portion of the king's meat.

Jeremiah 32:27 Behold, I am the LORD, the God of all flesh: is there anything too hard for me?

See also: Skin

GROIN

Deuteronomy 28:27 The LORD will smite thee with the botch of Egypt, and with the emerods, and with the scab, and with the itch, whereof thou canst not be healed.

Proverbs 31:17 She girdeth her loins with strength, and strengtheneth her arms.

Ephesians 6:14 Stand therefore, having your loins girt about with truth, and having on the breastplate of righteousness;

See also: Abdomen/Legs/Reproductive system

GUMS - see: Mouth

HAIR

Luke 21:18 But there shall not a hair of your head perish.

Luke 12:7 But even the very hairs of your head are all numbered. Fear not therefore: ye are of more value than many sparrows.

2 Samuel 14:11 Then said she, I pray thee, let the king remember the LORD thy God, that thou wouldest not suffer the revengers of blood to destroy any more, lest they destroy my son. And he said, As the LORD liveth, there shall not one hair of thy son fall to the earth.

2 Samuel 14:25 But in all Israel there was none to be so much praised as Absalom for his beauty: from the sole of his foot even to the crown of his head there was no blemish in him.

2 Samuel 14:26 And when he polled his head, (for it was at every year's end that he polled it: because the hair was heavy on him, therefore he polled it:) he weighed the hair of his head at two hundred shekels after the king's weight.

HANDS

Deuteronomy 33:7 And this is the blessing of Judah: and he said, Hear, LORD, the voice of Judah, and bring him unto his people: let his hands be sufficient for him; and be thou a help to him from his enemies.

Job 4:3 Behold, thou hast instructed many, and thou hast strengthened the weak hands.

THE SECRET TO THE HEALING POWER

Nehemiah 6:7 And thou hast also appointed prophets to preach of thee at Jerusalem, saying, There is a king in Judah: and now shall it be reported to the king according to these words. Come now therefore, and let us take counsel together.

Psalms 144:1 A Psalm of David. Blessed be the LORD my strength, which teacheth my hands to war, and my fingers to fight:

Isaiah 41:13 For I the LORD thy God will hold thy right hand, saying unto thee, Fear not; I will help thee.

Isaiah 35:3 Strengthen ye the weak hands, and confirm the feeble knees.

Mark 3:3 And he saith unto the man which had the withered hand, Stand forth.

Mark 3:5 And when he had looked round about on them with anger, being grieved for the hardness of their hearts, he saith unto the man, Stretch forth thine hand. And he stretched it out: and his hand was restored whole as the other.

See also: Arms/Arthritis

HEART

Psalms 73:26 My flesh and my heart failed: but God is the strength of my heart, and my portion forever.

Deuteronomy 28:61 Also every sickness, and every plague, which is not written in the book of this law, them will the LORD bring upon thee, until thou be destroyed.

Deuteronomy 28:65 And among these nations shalt thou find no ease, neither shall the sole of thy foot have rest: but the LORD shall give thee there a trembling heart, and failing of eyes, and sorrow of mind:

Galatians 3:13 Christ hath redeemed us from the curse of the law, being made a curse for us: for it is written, Cursed is every one that hangeth on a tree:

Psalms 147:3 He healeth the broken in heart, and bindeth up their wounds.

Psalms 22:26 The meek shall eat and be satisfied: they shall praise the LORD that seek him: your heart shall live forever.

Psalms 27:14 Wait on the LORD: be of good courage, and he shall strengthen thine heart: wait, I say, on the LORD.

See also: Blood HIPS

Song of Solomon 5:15 His legs are as pillars of marble, set upon sockets of fine gold: his countenance is as Lebanon, excellent as the cedars.

Song of Solomon 7:1 How beautiful are thy feet with shoes, O prince's daughter! the joints of thy thighs are like jewels, the work of the hands of a cunning workman.

See also: Knees/Legs/Arthritis

HORMONES - See: Reproductive system

IMMUNE SYSTEM

Romans 8:2 For the law of the Spirit of life in Christ Jesus hath made me free from the law of sin and death.

Psalms 91:5 Thou shalt not be afraid for the terror by night; nor for the arrow that flieth by day;

Psalms 91:6 Nor for the pestilence that walketh in darkness; nor for the destruction that wasteth at noonday.

Psalms 91:7 A thousand shall fall at thy side, and ten thousand at thy right hand; but it shall not come nigh thee.

Psalms 91:8 Only with thine eyes shalt thou behold and see the reward of the wicked.

Psalms 91:9 Because thou hast made the LORD, which is my refuge, even the most High, thy habitation;

Psalms 91:10 There shall no evil befall thee, neither shall any plague come nigh thy dwelling.

Exodus 11:7 But against any of the children of Israel shall not a dog move his tongue, against man or beast: that ye may know how that the LORD doth put a difference between the Egyptians and Israel.

Psalms 3:3 But thou, O LORD, art a shield for me; my glory, and the lifter up of mine head.

Isaiah 4:4 When the Lord shall have washed away the filth of the daughters of Zion, and shall have purged the blood of Jerusalem from the midst thereof by the spirit of judgment, and by the spirit of burning.

Isaiah 4:5 And the LORD will create upon every dwelling place of mount Zion, and upon her assemblies, a cloud and smoke by day, and the shining of a flaming fire by night: for upon all the glory shall be a defence.

Proverbs 30:5 Every word of God is pure: he is a shield unto them that put their trust in him.

Deuteronomy 28:21 The LORD shall make the pestilence cleave unto thee, until he have consumed thee from off the land, whither thou goest to possess it.

Galatian 3:13 Christ hath redeemed us from the curse of the law, being made a curse for us: for it is written, Cursed is every one that hangeth on a tree:

See also: Blood/Poisoning

JAW

Hosea 11:3 I taught Ephraim also to go, taking them by their arms; but they knew not that I healed them.

Hosea 11:4 I drew them with cords of a man, with bands of love: and I was to them as they that take off the yoke on their jaws, and I laid meat unto them.

See also: Mouth

JOINTS - see: Arthritis (specific body part affected)

KIDNEYS

Deuteronomy 28:61 Also every sickness, and every plague, which is not written in the book of this law, them will the LORD bring upon thee, until thou be destroyed.

Galatians 3:13 Christ hath redeemed us from the curse of the law, being made a curse for us: for it is written, Cursed is every one that hangeth on a tree:

See also: Blood/Infection

KNEES

Job 4:4 Thy words have upholden him that was falling, and thou hast strengthened the feeble knees.

Isaiah 35:3 Strengthen ye the weak hands, and confirm the feeble knees.

Hebrews 12:12 Wherefore lift up the hands which hang down, and the feeble knees;

Deuteronomy 28:35 The LORD shall smite thee in the knees, and in the legs, with a sore botch that cannot be healed, from the sole of thy foot unto the top of thy head.

Galatian 3:13 Christ hath redeemed us from the curse of the law, being made a curse for us: for it is written, Cursed is every one that hangeth on a tree:

See also: Legs/Arthritis LEGS

Isaiah 35:6 Then shall the lame man leap as a hart, and the tongue of the dumb sing: for in the wilderness shall waters break out, and streams in the desert.

Samuel 2:4 The bows of the mighty men are broken, and they that stumbled are girded with strength.

Song of Solomon 5:15 His legs are as pillars of marble, set upon sockets of fine gold: his countenance is as Lebanon, excellent as the cedars.

Song of Solomon 7:1 How beautiful are thy feet with shoes, O prince's daughter! the joints of thy thighs are like jewels, the work of the hands of a cunning workman.

Zechariah 10:12 And I will strengthen them in the LORD; and they shall walk up and down in his name, saith the LORD.

Hebrews 12:13 And make straight paths for your feet, lest that which is lame be turned out of the way; but let it rather be healed.

Deuteronomy 28:35 The LORD shall smite thee in the knees, and in the legs, with a sore botch that cannot be healed, from the sole of thy foot unto the top of thy head.

Galatians 3:13 Christ hath redeemed us from the curse of the law, being made a curse for us: for it is written, Cursed is every one that hangeth on a tree:

See also: Hips/Knees/Arthritis/Paralysis LIPS—see: Mouth

LIVER

Deuteronomy 28:22 The LORD shall smite thee with a consumption, and with a fever, and with an inflammation, and with an extreme burning, and with the sword, and with blasting, and with mildew; and they shall pursue thee until thou perish.

Galatians 3:13 Christ hath redeemed us from the curse of the law, being made a curse for us: for it is written, Cursed is every one that hangeth on a tree:

See also: Abdomen/ Immune/ Blood/ Flesh/ Poisoning/ Inflammation/ Jaundice

LUNGS - see: Respiratory System

MOUTH - Lips/Gums/Taste Buds/Tongue

Psalms 103:5 Who satisfieth thy mouth with good things; so that thy youth is renewed like the eagle's.

THE SECRET TO THE HEALING POWER

Song of Solomon 7:9 And the roof of thy mouth like the best wine for my beloved, that goeth down sweetly, causing the lips of those that are asleep to speak.

Proverbs 12:18 There is that Spaeth like the piercings of a sword: but the tongue of the wise is health.

Proverbs 12:19 The lip of truth shall be established forever: but a lying tongue is but for a moment.

Proverbs 8:6 Hear; for I will speak of excellent things; and the opening of my lips shall be right things.

Proverbs 8:7 For my mouth shall speak truth; and wickedness is an abomination to my lips.

Proverbs 8:8 All the words of my mouth are in righteousness; there is nothing froward or perverse in them.

Psalms 51:15 O Lord, open thou my lips; and my mouth shall shew forth thy praise.

Song of Solomon 4:11 Thy lips, O my spouse, drop as the honeycomb: honey and milk are under thy tongue; and the smell of thy garments is like the smell of Lebanon.

Job 6:6 Can that which is unsavoury be eaten without salt? or is there any taste in the white of an egg?

Job 6:30 Is there iniquity in my tongue? cannot my taste discern perverse things?

Deuteronomy 28:27 The LORD will smite thee with the botch of Egypt, and with the emerods, and with the scab, and with the itch, whereof thou canst not be healed.

Deuteronomy 28:61 Also every sickness, and every plague, which is not written in the book of this law, them will the LORD bring upon thee, until thou be destroyed.

Galatians 3:13 Christ hath redeemed us from the curse of the law, being made a curse for us: for it is written, Cursed is every one that hangeth on a tree:

See also: Digestion/Teeth/Speech disorders

MUSCLES—see: Sinews/Skin/Flesh/Paralysis

NECK

Song of Solomon 4:4 Thy neck is like the tower of David builded for an armoury, whereon there hang a thousand bucklers, all shields of mighty men.

Song of Solomon 7:4 Thy neck is as a tower of ivory; thine eyes like the fishpools in Heshbon, by the gate of Bathrabbim: thy nose is as the tower of Lebanon which looketh toward Damascus.

Isaiah 10:27 And it shall come to pass in that day, that his burden shall be taken away from off thy shoulder, and his yoke from off thy neck, and the yoke shall be destroyed because of the anointing.

See also: Back/ Bones/ Sinews/ Shoulder

NERVOUS SYSTEM (BRAIN)

John 1:5 And the light shineth in darkness; and the darkness comprehended it not.

Thessalonians 3:1 Finally, brethren, pray for us, that the word of the Lord may have free course, and be glorified, even as it is with you:

Job 19:8 He hath fenced up my way that I cannot pass, and he hath set darkness in my paths.

THE SECRET TO THE HEALING POWER

Proverbs 12:28 In the way of righteousness is life; and in the pathway thereof there is no death.

Isaiah 58:11 And the LORD shall guide thee continually, and satisfy thy soul in drought, and make fat thy bones: and thou shalt be like a watered garden, and like a spring of water, whose waters fail not.

Isaiah 58:12 And they that shall be of thee shall build the old waste places: thou shalt raise up the foundations of many generations; and thou shalt be called, The repairer of the breach, The restorer of paths to dwell in.

Deuteronomy 28:61 Also every sickness, and every plague, which is not written in the book of this law, them will the LORD bring upon thee, until thou be destroyed.

Galatians 3:13 Christ hath redeemed us from the curse of the law, being made a curse for us: for it is written, Cursed is every one that hangeth on a tree:

Luke 18:27 And he said, The things which are impossible with men are possible with God.

Mark 9:23 Jesus said unto him, if thou canst believe, all things are possible to him that believeth.

Jeremiah 32:27 Behold, I am the LORD, the God of all flesh: is there anything too hard for me?

See also: Paralysis/Mental health/Memory

NOSE

Song of Solomon 7:4 Thy neck is as a tower of ivory; thine eyes like the fishpools in Heshbon, by the gate of Bathrabbim: thy nose is as the tower of Lebanon which looketh toward Damascus.

Genesis 2:7 And the LORD God formed man of the dust of the ground, and breathed into his nostrils the breath of life; and man became a living soul.

See also: Respiratory system

OVARY—see: Reproductive system/Abdomen/Flesh

PROSTATE—see: Reproductive system/Abdomen/Flesh

QUADRICEPS (THIGH MUSCLE) See: Legs/Groin

REPRODUCTIVE SYSTEM

Deuteronomy 7:9 Know therefore that the LORD thy God, he is God, the faithful God, which keepeth covenant and mercy with them that love him and keep his commandments to a thousand generations;

Deuteronomy 7:12 Wherefore it shall come to pass, if ye hearken to these judgments, and keep, and do them, that the LORD thy God shall keep unto thee the covenant and the mercy which he sware unto thy fathers:

Deuteronomy 7:14 Thou shalt be blessed above all people: there shall not be male or female barren among you, or among your cattle.

Deuteronomy 7:15 And the LORD will take away from thee all sickness, and will put none of the evil diseases of Egypt, which thou knowest, upon thee; but will lay them upon all them that hate thee.

Deuteronomy 28:18 Cursed shall be the fruit of thy body, and the fruit of thy land, the increase of thy kine, and the flocks of thy sheep.

Deuteronomy 28:61 Also every sickness, and every plague, which is not written in the book of this law, them will the LORD bring upon thee, until thou be destroyed.

Galatians 3:13 Christ hath redeemed us from the curse of the law, being made a curse for us: for it is written, Cursed is every one that hangeth on a tree:

See also: Hereditary Diseases

RESPIRATORY SYSTEM

Genesis 2:7 And the LORD God formed man of the dust of the ground, and breathed into his nostrils the breath of life; and man became a living soul.

Act 17:25 Neither is worshipped with men's hands, as though he needed anything, seeing he giveth to all life, and breath, and all things;

Isaiah 42:5 Thus saith God the LORD, he that created the heavens, and stretched them out; he that spread forth the earth, and that which cometh out of it; he that giveth breath unto the people upon it, and spirit to them that walk therein:

Ezekiel 37:5 Thus saith the Lord GOD unto these bones; Behold, I will cause breath to enter into you, and ye shall live:

Ezekiel 37:6 And I will lay sinews upon you, and will bring up flesh upon you, and cover you with skin, and put breath in you, and ye shall live; and ye shall know that I am the LORD.

Ezekiel 37:9 Then said he unto me, Prophesy unto the wind, prophesy, son of man, and say to the wind, Thus saith the Lord GOD; Come from the four winds, O breath, and breathe upon these slain, that they may live.

Ezekiel 37:10 So I prophesied as he commanded me, and the breath came into them, and they lived, and stood up upon their feet, an exceeding great army.

Lamentations 3:56 Thou hast heard my voice: hide not thine ear at my breathing, at my cry.

Deuteronomy 28:22 The LORD shall smite thee with a consumption, and with a fever, and with an inflammation, and with an extreme burning, and with the sword, and with blasting, and with mildew; and they shall pursue thee until thou perish.

Deuteronomy 28:61 Also every sickness, and every plague, which is not written in the book of this law, them will the LORD bring upon thee, until thou be destroyed.

Galatians 3:13 Christ hath redeemed us from the curse of the law, being made a curse for us: for it is written, Cursed is every one that hangeth on a tree:

See also: Nose

SHOULDER

Isaiah 10:27 And it shall come to pass in that day, that his burden shall be taken away from off thy shoulder, and his yoke from off thy neck, and the yoke shall be destroyed because of the anointing.

See also: Back/ Neck/ Bones/ Sinews

SKIN

Job 10:11 Thou hast clothed me with skin and flesh, and hast fenced me with bones and sinews.

Job 10:12 Thou hast granted me life and favour, and thy visitation hath preserved my spirit.

Deuteronomy 28:27 The LORD will smite thee with the botch of Egypt, and with the emerods, and with the scab, and with the itch, whereof thou canst not be healed.

Deuteronomy 28:35 The LORD shall smite thee in the knees, and in the legs, with a sore botch that cannot be healed, from the sole of thy foot unto the top of thy head.

Galatians 3:13 Christ hath redeemed us from the curse of the law, being made a curse for us: for it is written, Cursed is every one that hangeth on a tree:

See also: Flesh/Sinews/Leprosy/Wounds/Infection/ Itch/Acne

SINEWS

Job 10:11 Thou hast clothed me with skin and flesh, and hast fenced me with bones and sinews.

Ezekiel 37:5 Thus saith the Lord GOD unto these bones; Behold, I will cause breath to enter into you, and ye shall live:

Ezekiel 37:6 And I will lay sinews upon you, and will bring up flesh upon you, and cover you with skin, and put breath in you, and ye shall live; and ye shall know that I am the LORD.

See also: Flesh/Skin

STOMACH—see: Abdomen

TEETH

Song of Solomon 4:2 Thy teeth are like a flock of sheep that are even shorn, which came up from the washing; whereof every one bear twins, and none is barren among them.

Song of Solomon 4:3 Thy lips are like a thread of scarlet, and thy speech is comely: thy temples are like a piece of a pomegranate within thy locks.

Deuteronomy 34:7 And Moses was a hundred and twenty years old when he died: his eye was not dim, nor his natural force abated.

See also: Bones/Mouth

TONGUE

Song of Solomon 4:11 Thy lips, O my spouse, drop as the honeycomb: honey and milk are under thy tongue; and the smell of thy garments is like the smell of Lebanon.

Proverbs 12:18 There is that speaketh like the piercings of a sword: but the tongue of the wise is health.

See also: Mouth

URINARY TRACT—see: Kidney/Infection

VEINS

Deuteronomy 28:61 Also every sickness, and every plague, which is not written in the book of this law, them will the LORD bring upon thee, until thou be destroyed.

Galatians 3:13 Christ hath redeemed us from the curse of the law, being made a curse for us: for it is written, Cursed is every one that hangeth on a tree:

See also: Blood/Inflammation

WRIST—see: Hand/Arthritis

X, Y, Z — (Male and Female chromosomes, zygote, fertilized egg)

See: Reproductive system/Hereditary diseases

Chapter 15
Supernatural Aftercare

Maintain Your Healing and Deliverance

The goal of this section is to provide spiritual care after being healed, delivered or touched by Jesus.

Once the power of God has touched you, it is our responsibility for maintaining our wholeness by applying the Word of God in the area of our healing and deliverance consistently until we have a knowing it is complete. We must fill our hearts and minds with the Word of God.

Remember!

No Word from GOD is Void of Power – Luke 1:37 ASV

God's Word is living and can be experienced by everyone who believes it. Jesus said unto him, if thou canst believe, All things are possible to them that believe! **Mark 9:23**

Isaiah 55:11 KJV – So shall my Word be that goeth forth out of my mouth: it shall not return unto Me void, but it shall accomplish that which I please, and it shall prosper in the thing whereto I sent it.

Matthew 12:43 KJV – When the unclean spirit is gone out of a man, he walketh through dry places, seeking rest, and findeth none.

Matthew 12:44 KJV – Then he saith, I will return into my house from whence I came out; and when he is come, he findeth it empty, swept, and garnished.

Tips on receiving and maintaining your healing and deliverance

- Apply the following to your life every day and believe what the Word says concerning your condition:
- Declare the Blood of Jesus over your life
- Stay away from negative words and environments that speak against your healing and deliverance
- Maintain a healthy diet and exercise
- Repent of bad habits in your life (example – overeating, etc.)
- Denounce illegal covenants with people, demonic rituals, etc.
- Repent of sins (commission and omission).
- Act on the Word of God every day
- Forgive others, forgive yourself, forgive your body.
- Pray in the Holy Spirit.
- Speak healing and deliverance Scriptures over your body that has been affected
- Worship and praise God daily
- Keep your mind on Jesus
- Married couples ensure that there is peace between you... so that your prayers are not hindered. **1 Peter 3:7**

When you need healing – you need faith! To activate and grow your faith for healing, the Word of God is a powerful tool for getting the truth down inside your spirit. Faith comes by hearing the Word of God—over and over and over again.

Matthew 4:4 – But he answered and said, It is written, Man shall not live by bread alone, but by every word that proceedeth out of the mouth of God.

1 Corinthians 6:19 – What? know ye not that your body is the temple of the Holy Ghost [which is] in you, which ye have of God, and ye are not your own?

1 Corinthians 10:31 – Whether therefore ye eat, or drink, or whatsoever ye do, do all to the glory of God.

Secondly, because we live in human bodies, we must also act upon the Word of God by taking care of ourselves by:

1 Corinthians 3:17 – If any man defile the temple of God, him shall God destroy; for the temple of God is holy, which [temple] ye are.

"To be spoken by mouth three times a day until faith comes, then once a day to maintain faith. If circumstances grow worse, double the dosage. There are no harmful side effects."

— **CHARLES CAPPS**

- Begin reading the Scriptures every day pertaining to your condition, no matter what you are feeling in your body.
- Meditate on the Word of God until you can see your healing manifested in your spirit man.
- Keep declaring the Word of God over your body, mind and spirit until you are healed, delivered or have the peace of God within.

(If you are under doctor's care, maintain your care until all symptons are gone.)

References

http://christianityinreallife.blogspot.com/2013/02/what-gods-voice-sounds-like-reported.html

http://phys.org/news/2013-02-cells-scientists-probe-human-high-frequency.html

http://www.ctvnews.ca/health/device-aims-for-early-detection-of-cancer-cells-by-identifying-their-sound-1.1420132

http://www.cwgministries.org/4keys/vid14keys.html?utm_source=4+Keys+to+Hearing+God's+Voice+Video+Training&utm_campaign=4_Keys_Vids_1&utm_medium=email

http://www.heavensinspirations.com/word-voice.html

http://www.msia.org/sound

http://www.nexneuro.com/media/pdf/dr-karel-jindrak.pdf

http://www.popsci.com/scitech/article/2008-01/do-cells-make-nois

https://greenmedicine.ie/school/images/Library/Emotions-and-Your-Nervous-System.pdf

https://www.webmd.com/back-pain/features/emotional-effects

Institute of HeartMath, www.heartmath.org.

Lipton, Bruce. The Biology of Belief, 2001.

Pert, Candace. "Your Body Is Your Subconscious Mind" (Audio CD), 1997.

Pert, Candace. Molecules of Emotion, 1997.

Made in the USA
Columbia, SC
26 June 2024

eee8a4fe-e1fe-4ee9-9960-ff54baf3fd9bR01